Hamlet

William Shakespeare

Large Student Annotation Edition:
Formatted with wide spacing and wide
margins for your own notes and responses

Formatting copyright Panda'sDen 2019

ISBN: 9781081956479

Dramatis Personae

Claudius, King of Denmark

Hamlet, son to the late, and nephew to the present king

Polonius, Lord Chamberlain

Horatio, friend to Hamlet

Laertes, son to Polonius

Voltimand, Cornelius, Rosencrantz, Guildenstern, Osric, a

Gentleman, courtiers

A Priest

Marcellus, Barnardo, officers

Francisco, a soldier

Reynaldo, servant to Polonius

Players

Two Clowns, grave-diggers

Fortinbras, Prince of Norway

A Captain

English Ambassadors

Gertrude, Queen of Denmark and mother to Hamlet

Ophelia, daughter to Polonius

Lords, Ladies, Officers, Soldiers, Sailors, Messengers, and other

Attendants

Ghost of Hamlet's Father

Scene: Denmark

ACT I

SCENE I. Elsinore. A platform before the castle.

FRANCISCO at his post. Enter to him BERNARDO

BERNARDO
Who's there?

FRANCISCO
Nay, answer me: stand, and unfold yourself.

BERNARDO
Long live the king!

FRANCISCO
Bernardo?

BERNARDO
He.

FRANCISCO
You come most carefully upon your hour.

BERNARDO
'Tis now struck twelve; get thee to bed, Francisco.

FRANCISCO
For this relief much thanks: 'tis bitter cold,

And I am sick at heart.

BERNARDO
Have you had quiet guard?

FRANCISCO
Not a mouse stirring.

BERNARDO
Well, good night.

If you do meet Horatio and Marcellus,

The rivals of my watch, bid them make haste.

FRANCISCO
I think I hear them. Stand, ho! Who's there?

Enter HORATIO and MARCELLUS

HORATIO
Friends to this ground.

MARCELLUS
And liegemen to the Dane.

FRANCISCO
Give you good night.

MARCELLUS
O, farewell, honest soldier:

Who hath relieved you?

FRANCISCO
Bernardo has my place.

Give you good night.

Exit

MARCELLUS
Holla! Bernardo!

BERNARDO
Say,

What, is Horatio there?

HORATIO
A piece of him.

BERNARDO
Welcome, Horatio: welcome, good Marcellus.

MARCELLUS
What, has this thing appear'd again to-night?

BERNARDO
I have seen nothing.

MARCELLUS
Horatio says 'tis but our fantasy,

And will not let belief take hold of him

Touching this dreaded sight, twice seen of us:

Therefore I have entreated him along

With us to watch the minutes of this night;

That if again this apparition come,

He may approve our eyes and speak to it.

HORATIO
Tush, tush, 'twill not appear.

BERNARDO
Sit down awhile;

And let us once again assail your ears,

That are so fortified against our story

What we have two nights seen.

HORATIO
Well, sit we down,

And let us hear Bernardo speak of this.

BERNARDO
Last night of all,

When yond same star that's westward from the pole

Had made his course to illume that part of heaven

Where now it burns, Marcellus and myself,

The bell then beating one,--

Enter Ghost

MARCELLUS

Peace, break thee off; look, where it comes again!

BERNARDO

In the same figure, like the king that's dead.

MARCELLUS

Thou art a scholar; speak to it, Horatio.

BERNARDO

Looks it not like the king? mark it, Horatio.

HORATIO

Most like: it harrows me with fear and wonder.

BERNARDO

It would be spoke to.

MARCELLUS

Question it, Horatio.

HORATIO

What art thou that usurp'st this time of night,

Together with that fair and warlike form

In which the majesty of buried Denmark

Did sometimes march? by heaven I charge thee, speak!

MARCELLUS

It is offended.

BERNARDO

See, it stalks away!

HORATIO

Stay! speak, speak! I charge thee, speak!

Exit Ghost

MARCELLUS

'Tis gone, and will not answer.

BERNARDO
How now, Horatio! you tremble and look pale:

Is not this something more than fantasy?

What think you on't?

HORATIO
Before my God, I might not this believe

Without the sensible and true avouch

Of mine own eyes.

MARCELLUS
Is it not like the king?

HORATIO
As thou art to thyself:

Such was the very armour he had on

When he the ambitious Norway combated;

So frown'd he once, when, in an angry parle,

He smote the sledded Polacks on the ice.

'Tis strange.

MARCELLUS
Thus twice before, and jump at this dead hour,

With martial stalk hath he gone by our watch.

HORATIO
In what particular thought to work I know not;

But in the gross and scope of my opinion,

This bodes some strange eruption to our state.

MARCELLUS

Good now, sit down, and tell me, he that knows,

Why this same strict and most observant watch

So nightly toils the subject of the land,

And why such daily cast of brazen cannon,

And foreign mart for implements of war;

Why such impress of shipwrights, whose sore task

Does not divide the Sunday from the week;

What might be toward, that this sweaty haste

Doth make the night joint-labourer with the day:

Who is't that can inform me?

HORATIO

That can I;

At least, the whisper goes so. Our last king,

Whose image even but now appear'd to us,

Was, as you know, by Fortinbras of Norway,

Thereto prick'd on by a most emulate pride,

Dared to the combat; in which our valiant Hamlet--

For so this side of our known world esteem'd him--

Did slay this Fortinbras; who by a seal'd compact,

Well ratified by law and heraldry,

Did forfeit, with his life, all those his lands

Which he stood seized of, to the conqueror:

Against the which, a moiety competent

Was gaged by our king; which had return'd

To the inheritance of Fortinbras,

Had he been vanquisher; as, by the same covenant,

And carriage of the article design'd,

His fell to Hamlet. Now, sir, young Fortinbras,

Of unimproved mettle hot and full,

Hath in the skirts of Norway here and there

Shark'd up a list of lawless resolutes,

For food and diet, to some enterprise

That hath a stomach in't; which is no other--

As it doth well appear unto our state--

But to recover of us, by strong hand

And terms compulsatory, those foresaid lands

So by his father lost: and this, I take it,

Is the main motive of our preparations,

The source of this our watch and the chief head

Of this post-haste and romage in the land.

BERNARDO
I think it be no other but e'en so:

Well may it sort that this portentous figure

Comes armed through our watch; so like the king

That was and is the question of these wars.

HORATIO

A mote it is to trouble the mind's eye.

In the most high and palmy state of Rome,

A little ere the mightiest Julius fell,

The graves stood tenantless and the sheeted dead

Did squeak and gibber in the Roman streets:

As stars with trains of fire and dews of blood,

Disasters in the sun; and the moist star

Upon whose influence Neptune's empire stands

Was sick almost to doomsday with eclipse:

And even the like precurse of fierce events,

As harbingers preceding still the fates

And prologue to the omen coming on,

Have heaven and earth together demonstrated

Unto our climatures and countrymen.--

But soft, behold! lo, where it comes again!

Re-enter Ghost

I'll cross it, though it blast me. Stay, illusion!

If thou hast any sound, or use of voice,

Speak to me:

If there be any good thing to be done,

That may to thee do ease and grace to me,

Speak to me:

Divine Right (handwritten marginal note)

Cock crows

If thou art privy to thy country's fate,

Which, happily, foreknowing may avoid, O, speak!

Or if thou hast uphoarded in thy life

Extorted treasure in the womb of earth,

For which, they say, you spirits oft walk in death,

Speak of it: stay, and speak! Stop it, Marcellus.

MARCELLUS
Shall I strike at it with my partisan?

HORATIO
Do, if it will not stand.

BERNARDO
'Tis here!

HORATIO
'Tis here!

MARCELLUS
'Tis gone!

Exit Ghost

We do it wrong, being so majestical,

To offer it the show of violence;

For it is, as the air, invulnerable,

And our vain blows malicious mockery.

BERNARDO
It was about to speak, when the cock crew.

HORATIO

And then it started like a guilty thing

Upon a fearful summons. I have heard,

The cock, that is the trumpet to the morn,

Doth with his lofty and shrill-sounding throat

Awake the god of day; and, at his warning,

Whether in sea or fire, in earth or air,

The extravagant and erring spirit hies

To his confine: and of the truth herein

This present object made probation.

MARCELLUS

It faded on the crowing of the cock.

Some say that ever 'gainst that season comes

Wherein our Saviour's birth is celebrated,

The bird of dawning singeth all night long:

And then, they say, no spirit dares stir abroad;

The nights are wholesome; then no planets strike,

No fairy takes, nor witch hath power to charm,

So hallow'd and so gracious is the time.

HORATIO

So have I heard and do in part believe it.

But, look, the morn, in russet mantle clad,

Walks o'er the dew of yon high eastward hill:

Break we our watch up; and by my advice,

Let us impart what we have seen to-night

Unto young Hamlet; for, upon my life,

This spirit, dumb to us, will speak to him. *foreshadowing*

Do you consent we shall acquaint him with it,

As needful in our loves, fitting our duty?

MARCELLUS
Let's do't, I pray; and I this morning know

Where we shall find him most conveniently.

Exeunt

<u>NOTES</u>

SCENE II. A room of state in the castle.

Enter KING CLAUDIUS, QUEEN GERTRUDE, HAMLET, POLONIUS,

LAERTES, VOLTIMAND, CORNELIUS, Lords, and Attendants

KING CLAUDIUS
Though yet of Hamlet our dear brother's death

The memory be green, and that it us befitted

To bear our hearts in grief and our whole kingdom

To be contracted in one brow of woe,

Yet so far hath discretion fought with nature

That we with wisest sorrow think on him,

Together with remembrance of ourselves.

Therefore our sometime sister, now our queen,

The imperial jointress to this warlike state,

Have we, as 'twere with a defeated joy,--

With an auspicious and a dropping eye,

With mirth in funeral and with dirge in marriage,

In equal scale weighing delight and dole,--

Taken to wife: nor have we herein barr'd

Your better wisdoms, which have freely gone

With this affair along. For all, our thanks.

Now follows, that you know, young Fortinbras,

Holding a weak supposal of our worth,

Or thinking by our late dear brother's death

Our state to be disjoint and out of frame,

Colleagued with the dream of his advantage,

He hath not fail'd to pester us with message,

Importing the surrender of those lands

Lost by his father, with all bonds of law,

To our most valiant brother. So much for him.

Now for ourself and for this time of meeting:

Thus much the business is: we have here writ

To Norway, uncle of young Fortinbras,--

Who, impotent and bed-rid, scarcely hears

Of this his nephew's purpose,--to suppress

His further gait herein; in that the levies,

The lists and full proportions, are all made

Out of his subject: and we here dispatch

You, good Cornelius, and you, Voltimand,

For bearers of this greeting to old Norway;

Giving to you no further personal power

To business with the king, more than the scope

Of these delated articles allow.

Farewell, and let your haste commend your duty.

CORNELIUS VOLTIMAND
In that and all things will we show our duty.

KING CLAUDIUS
We doubt it nothing: heartily farewell.

Exeunt VOLTIMAND and CORNELIUS

And now, Laertes, what's the news with you?

You told us of some suit; what is't, Laertes?

You cannot speak of reason to the Dane,

And loose your voice: what wouldst thou beg, Laertes,

That shall not be my offer, not thy asking?

The head is not more native to the heart,

The hand more instrumental to the mouth,

Than is the throne of Denmark to thy father.

What wouldst thou have, Laertes?

LAERTES
My dread lord,

Your leave and favour to return to France;

From whence though willingly I came to Denmark,

To show my duty in your coronation,

Yet now, I must confess, that duty done,

My thoughts and wishes bend again toward France

And bow them to your gracious leave and pardon.

KING CLAUDIUS
Have you your father's leave? What says Polonius?

LORD POLONIUS
He hath, my lord, wrung from me my slow leave

By laboursome petition, and at last

Upon his will I seal'd my hard consent:

I do beseech you, give him leave to go.

KING CLAUDIUS
Take thy fair hour, Laertes; time be thine,

And thy best graces spend it at thy will!

But now, my cousin Hamlet, and my son,--

HAMLET
[Aside] A little more than kin, and less than kind.

KING CLAUDIUS
How is it that the clouds still hang on you?

HAMLET
Not so, my lord; I am too much i' the sun.

QUEEN GERTRUDE
Good Hamlet, cast thy nighted colour off,

And let thine eye look like a friend on Denmark.

Do not for ever with thy vailed lids

Seek for thy noble father in the dust:

Thou know'st 'tis common; all that lives must die,

Passing through nature to eternity.

HAMLET
Ay, madam, it is common.

QUEEN GERTRUDE
If it be,

Why seems it so particular with thee?

HAMLET
Seems, madam! nay it is; I know not 'seems.'

'Tis not alone my inky cloak, good mother,

Nor customary suits of solemn black,

Nor windy suspiration of forced breath,

No, nor the fruitful river in the eye,

Nor the dejected 'havior of the visage,

Together with all forms, moods, shapes of grief,

That can denote me truly: these indeed seem,

For they are actions that a man might play:

But I have that within which passeth show;

These but the trappings and the suits of woe.

KING CLAUDIUS
'Tis sweet and commendable in your nature, Hamlet,

To give these mourning duties to your father:

But, you must know, your father lost a father;

That father lost, lost his, and the survivor bound

In filial obligation for some term

To do obsequious sorrow: but to persever

In obstinate condolement is a course

Of impious stubbornness; 'tis unmanly grief;

It shows a will most incorrect to heaven,

A heart unfortified, a mind impatient,

An understanding simple and unschool'd:

For what we know must be and is as common

As any the most vulgar thing to sense,

Why should we in our peevish opposition

Take it to heart? Fie! 'tis a fault to heaven,

A fault against the dead, a fault to nature,

To reason most absurd: whose common theme

Is death of fathers, and who still hath cried,

From the first corse till he that died to-day,

'This must be so.' We pray you, throw to earth

This unprevailing woe, and think of us

As of a father: for let the world take note,

You are the most immediate to our throne;

And with no less nobility of love

Than that which dearest father bears his son,

Do I impart toward you. For your intent

In going back to school in Wittenberg,

It is most retrograde to our desire:

And we beseech you, bend you to remain

Here, in the cheer and comfort of our eye,

Our chiefest courtier, cousin, and our son.

He is telling him to get over it

QUEEN GERTRUDE
Let not thy mother lose her prayers, Hamlet:

I pray thee, stay with us; go not to Wittenberg.

HAMLET
I shall in all my best obey you, madam.

KING CLAUDIUS
Why, 'tis a loving and a fair reply:

Be as ourself in Denmark. Madam, come;

This gentle and unforced accord of Hamlet

Sits smiling to my heart: in grace whereof,

No jocund health that Denmark drinks to-day,

But the great cannon to the clouds shall tell,

And the king's rouse the heavens all bruit again,

Re-speaking earthly thunder. Come away.

Exeunt all but HAMLET

HAMLET
O, that this too too solid flesh would melt

Thaw and resolve itself into a dew!

Or that the Everlasting had not fix'd

His canon 'gainst self-slaughter! O God! God!

How weary, stale, flat and unprofitable,

Seem to me all the uses of this world!

Fie on't! ah fie! 'tis an unweeded garden,

That grows to seed; things rank and gross in nature

Possess it merely. That it should come to this!

But two months dead: nay, not so much, not two:

So excellent a king; that was, to this,

Hyperion to a satyr; so loving to my mother

That he might not beteem the winds of heaven

Visit her face too roughly. Heaven and earth!

Must I remember? why, she would hang on him,

As if increase of appetite had grown

By what it fed on: and yet, within a month--

Let me not think on't--Frailty, thy name is woman!--

A little month, or ere those shoes were old

With which she follow'd my poor father's body,

Like Niobe, all tears:--why she, even she--

O, God! a beast, that wants discourse of reason,

Would have mourn'd longer--married with my uncle,

My father's brother, but no more like my father

Than I to Hercules: within a month:

Ere yet the salt of most unrighteous tears

Had left the flushing in her galled eyes,

She married. O, most wicked speed, to post

With such dexterity to incestuous sheets!

why did he die
- Hamlet

he doesn't like his mom for her actions

It is not nor it cannot come to good:

But break, my heart; for I must hold my tongue.

Enter HORATIO, MARCELLUS, and BERNARDO

HORATIO
Hail to your lordship!

HAMLET
I am glad to see you well:

Horatio,--or I do forget myself.

HORATIO
The same, my lord, and your poor servant ever.

HAMLET
Sir, my good friend; I'll change that name with you:

And what make you from Wittenberg, Horatio? Marcellus?

MARCELLUS
My good lord--

HAMLET
I am very glad to see you. Good even, sir.

But what, in faith, make you from Wittenberg?

HORATIO
A truant disposition, good my lord.

HAMLET
I would not hear your enemy say so,

Nor shall you do mine ear that violence,

To make it truster of your own report

Against yourself: I know you are no truant.

But what is your affair in Elsinore?

We'll teach you to drink deep ere you depart.

HORATIO
My lord, I came to see your father's funeral.

HAMLET
I pray thee, do not mock me, fellow-student;

I think it was to see my mother's wedding.

HORATIO
Indeed, my lord, it follow'd hard upon.

HAMLET
Thrift, thrift, Horatio! the funeral baked meats

Did coldly furnish forth the marriage tables.

Would I had met my dearest foe in heaven

Or ever I had seen that day, Horatio!

My father!--methinks I see my father.

HORATIO
Where, my lord?

HAMLET
In my mind's eye, Horatio.

HORATIO
I saw him once; he was a goodly king.

HAMLET
He was a man, take him for all in all,

I shall not look upon his like again.

HORATIO
My lord, I think I saw him yesternight.

HAMLET
Saw? who?

HORATIO
My lord, the king your father.

HAMLET
The king my father!

HORATIO
Season your admiration for awhile

With an attent ear, till I may deliver,

Upon the witness of these gentlemen,

This marvel to you.

HAMLET
For God's love, let me hear.

HORATIO
Two nights together had these gentlemen,

Marcellus and Bernardo, on their watch,

In the dead vast and middle of the night,

Been thus encounter'd. A figure like your father,

Armed at point exactly, cap-a-pe,

Appears before them, and with solemn march

Goes slow and stately by them: thrice he walk'd

By their oppress'd and fear-surprised eyes,

Within his truncheon's length; whilst they, distilled

Almost to jelly with the act of fear,

Stand dumb and speak not to him. This to me

In dreadful secrecy impart they did;

And I with them the third night kept the watch;

Where, as they had deliver'd, both in time,

Form of the thing, each word made true and good,

The apparition comes: I knew your father;

These hands are not more like.

HAMLET
But where was this?

MARCELLUS
My lord, upon the platform where we watch'd.

HAMLET
Did you not speak to it?

HORATIO
My lord, I did;

But answer made it none: yet once methought

It lifted up its head and did address

Itself to motion, like as it would speak;

But even then the morning cock crew loud,

And at the sound it shrunk in haste away,

And vanish'd from our sight.

HAMLET
'Tis very strange.

HORATIO
As I do live, my honour'd lord, 'tis true;

And we did think it writ down in our duty

To let you know of it.

HAMLET
Indeed, indeed, sirs, but this troubles me.

Hold you the watch to-night?

MARCELLUS BERNARDO
We do, my lord.

HAMLET
Arm'd, say you?

MARCELLUS BERNARDO
Arm'd, my lord.

HAMLET
From top to toe?

MARCELLUS BERNARDO
My lord, from head to foot.

HAMLET
Then saw you not his face?

HORATIO
O, yes, my lord; he wore his beaver up.

HAMLET
What, look'd he frowningly?

HORATIO
A countenance more in sorrow than in anger.

HAMLET
Pale or red?

HORATIO
Nay, very pale.

HAMLET
And fix'd his eyes upon you?

HORATIO
Most constantly.

HAMLET
I would I had been there.

HORATIO
It would have much amazed you.

HAMLET
Very like, very like. Stay'd it long?

HORATIO
While one with moderate haste might tell a hundred.

MARCELLUS BERNARDO
Longer, longer.

HORATIO
Not when I saw't.

HAMLET
His beard was grizzled--no?

HORATIO
It was, as I have seen it in his life,

A sable silver'd.

HAMLET
I will watch to-night;

Perchance 'twill walk again.

HORATIO
I warrant it will.

HAMLET
If it assume my noble father's person,

I'll speak to it, though hell itself should gape

And bid me hold my peace. I pray you all,

If you have hitherto conceal'd this sight,

Let it be tenable in your silence still;

And whatsoever else shall hap to-night,

Give it an understanding, but no tongue:

I will requite your loves. So, fare you well:

Upon the platform, 'twixt eleven and twelve,

I'll visit you.

All
Our duty to your honour.

HAMLET
Your loves, as mine to you: farewell.

Exeunt all but HAMLET
My father's spirit in arms! all is not well;

I doubt some foul play: would the night were come!

Till then sit still, my soul: foul deeds will rise,

Though all the earth o'erwhelm them, to men's eyes.

Exit

<u>NOTES</u>

SCENE III. A room in Polonius' house.

Enter LAERTES and OPHELIA

LAERTES
My necessaries are embark'd: farewell:

And, sister, as the winds give benefit

And convoy is assistant, do not sleep,

But let me hear from you.

OPHELIA
Do you doubt that?

LAERTES
For Hamlet and the trifling of his favour,

Hold it a fashion and a toy in blood,

A violet in the youth of primy nature,

Forward, not permanent, sweet, not lasting,

The perfume and suppliance of a minute; No more.

OPHELIA
No more but so?

LAERTES
Think it no more;

For nature, crescent, does not grow alone

In thews and bulk, but, as this temple waxes,

The inward service of the mind and soul

Grows wide withal. Perhaps he loves you now,

And now no soil nor cautel doth besmirch

The virtue of his will: but you must fear,

His greatness weigh'd, his will is not his own;

For he himself is subject to his birth:

He may not, as unvalued persons do,

Carve for himself; for on his choice depends

The safety and health of this whole state;

And therefore must his choice be circumscribed

Unto the voice and yielding of that body

Whereof he is the head. Then if he says he loves you,

It fits your wisdom so far to believe it

As he in his particular act and place

May give his saying deed; which is no further

Than the main voice of Denmark goes withal.

Then weigh what loss your honour may sustain,

If with too credent ear you list his songs,

Or lose your heart, or your chaste treasure open

To his unmaster'd importunity.

Fear it, Ophelia, fear it, my dear sister,

And keep you in the rear of your affection,

Out of the shot and danger of desire.

The chariest maid is prodigal enough,

If she unmask her beauty to the moon:

Virtue itself 'scapes not calumnious strokes:

The canker galls the infants of the spring,

Too oft before their buttons be disclosed,

And in the morn and liquid dew of youth

Contagious blastments are most imminent.

Be wary then; best safety lies in fear:

Youth to itself rebels, though none else near.

OPHELIA
I shall the effect of this good lesson keep,

As watchman to my heart. But, good my brother,

Do not, as some ungracious pastors do,

Show me the steep and thorny way to heaven;

Whiles, like a puff'd and reckless libertine,

Himself the primrose path of dalliance treads,

And recks not his own rede.

LAERTES
O, fear me not.

I stay too long: but here my father comes.

Enter POLONIUS

A double blessing is a double grace,

Occasion smiles upon a second leave.

LORD POLONIUS
Yet here, Laertes! aboard, aboard, for shame!

The wind sits in the shoulder of your sail,

And you are stay'd for. There; my blessing with thee!

And these few precepts in thy memory

See thou character. Give thy thoughts no tongue,

Nor any unproportioned thought his act.

Be thou familiar, but by no means vulgar.

Those friends thou hast, and their adoption tried,

Grapple them to thy soul with hoops of steel;

But do not dull thy palm with entertainment

Of each new-hatch'd, unfledged comrade. Beware

Of entrance to a quarrel, but being in,

Bear't that the opposed may beware of thee.

Give every man thy ear, but few thy voice;

Take each man's censure, but reserve thy judgment.

Costly thy habit as thy purse can buy,

But not express'd in fancy; rich, not gaudy;

For the apparel oft proclaims the man,

And they in France of the best rank and station

Are of a most select and generous chief in that.

Neither a borrower nor a lender be;

For loan oft loses both itself and friend,

And borrowing dulls the edge of husbandry.

This above all: to thine ownself be true,

And it must follow, as the night the day,

Thou canst not then be false to any man.

Farewell: my blessing season this in thee!

LAERTES
Most humbly do I take my leave, my lord.

LORD POLONIUS
The time invites you; go; your servants tend.

LAERTES
Farewell, Ophelia; and remember well

What I have said to you.

OPHELIA
'Tis in my memory lock'd,

And you yourself shall keep the key of it.

LAERTES
Farewell.

Exit

LORD POLONIUS
What is't, Ophelia, be hath said to you?

OPHELIA
So please you, something touching the Lord Hamlet.

LORD POLONIUS
Marry, well bethought:

'Tis told me, he hath very oft of late

Given private time to you; and you yourself

Have of your audience been most free and bounteous:

If it be so, as so 'tis put on me,

And that in way of caution, I must tell you,

You do not understand yourself so clearly

As it behoves my daughter and your honour.

What is between you? give me up the truth.

OPHELIA
He hath, my lord, of late made many tenders

Of his affection to me.

LORD POLONIUS
Affection! pooh! you speak like a green girl,

Unsifted in such perilous circumstance.

Do you believe his tenders, as you call them?

OPHELIA
I do not know, my lord, what I should think.

LORD POLONIUS
Marry, I'll teach you: think yourself a baby;

That you have ta'en these tenders for true pay,

Which are not sterling. Tender yourself more dearly;

Or--not to crack the wind of the poor phrase,

Running it thus--you'll tender me a fool.

OPHELIA
My lord, he hath importuned me with love

In honourable fashion.

LORD POLONIUS
Ay, fashion you may call it; go to, go to.

OPHELIA
And hath given countenance to his speech, my lord,

With almost all the holy vows of heaven.

LORD POLONIUS
Ay, springes to catch woodcocks. I do know,

When the blood burns, how prodigal the soul

Lends the tongue vows: these blazes, daughter,

Giving more light than heat, extinct in both,

Even in their promise, as it is a-making,

You must not take for fire. From this time

Be somewhat scanter of your maiden presence;

Set your entreatments at a higher rate

Than a command to parley. For Lord Hamlet,

Believe so much in him, that he is young

And with a larger tether may he walk

Than may be given you: in few, Ophelia,

Do not believe his vows; for they are brokers,

Not of that dye which their investments show,

But mere implorators of unholy suits,

Breathing like sanctified and pious bawds,

The better to beguile. This is for all:

I would not, in plain terms, from this time forth,

Have you so slander any moment leisure,

As to give words or talk with the Lord Hamlet.

Look to't, I charge you: come your ways.

OPHELIA
I shall obey, my lord.

Exeunt

<u>*NOTES*</u>

SCENE IV. The platform.

Enter HAMLET, HORATIO, and MARCELLUS

HAMLET
The air bites shrewdly; it is very cold.

HORATIO
It is a nipping and an eager air.

HAMLET
What hour now?

HORATIO
I think it lacks of twelve.

HAMLET
No, it is struck.

HORATIO
Indeed? I heard it not: then it draws near the season

Wherein the spirit held his wont to walk.

A flourish of trumpets, and ordnance shot off, within

What does this mean, my lord?

HAMLET
The king doth wake to-night and takes his rouse,

Keeps wassail, and the swaggering up-spring reels;

And, as he drains his draughts of Rhenish down,

The kettle-drum and trumpet thus bray out

The triumph of his pledge.

HORATIO
Is it a custom?

HAMLET
Ay, marry, is't:

But to my mind, though I am native here

And to the manner born, it is a custom

More honour'd in the breach than the observance.

This heavy-headed revel east and west

Makes us traduced and tax'd of other nations:

They clepe us drunkards, and with swinish phrase

Soil our addition; and indeed it takes

From our achievements, though perform'd at height,

The pith and marrow of our attribute.

So, oft it chances in particular men,

That for some vicious mole of nature in them,

As, in their birth--wherein they are not guilty,

Since nature cannot choose his origin--

By the o'ergrowth of some complexion,

Oft breaking down the pales and forts of reason,

Or by some habit that too much o'er-leavens

The form of plausive manners, that these men,

Carrying, I say, the stamp of one defect,

Being nature's livery, or fortune's star,--

Their virtues else--be they as pure as grace,

As infinite as man may undergo--

Shall in the general censure take corruption

From that particular fault: the dram of eale

Doth all the noble substance of a doubt

To his own scandal.

HORATIO
Look, my lord, it comes!

Enter Ghost

HAMLET
Angels and ministers of grace defend us!

Be thou a spirit of health or goblin damn'd,

Bring with thee airs from heaven or blasts from hell,

Be thy intents wicked or charitable,

Thou comest in such a questionable shape

That I will speak to thee: I'll call thee Hamlet,

King, father, royal Dane: O, answer me!

Let me not burst in ignorance; but tell

Why thy canonized bones, hearsed in death,

Have burst their cerements; why the sepulchre,

Wherein we saw thee quietly inurn'd,

Hath oped his ponderous and marble jaws,

To cast thee up again. What may this mean,

That thou, dead corse, again in complete steel

Revisit'st thus the glimpses of the moon,

Making night hideous; and we fools of nature

So horridly to shake our disposition

With thoughts beyond the reaches of our souls?

Say, why is this? wherefore? what should we do?

Ghost beckons HAMLET

HORATIO
It beckons you to go away with it,

As if it some impartment did desire

To you alone.

MARCELLUS
Look, with what courteous action

It waves you to a more removed ground:

But do not go with it.

HORATIO
No, by no means.

HAMLET
It will not speak; then I will follow it.

HORATIO
Do not, my lord.

HAMLET
Why, what should be the fear?

I do not set my life in a pin's fee;

And for my soul, what can it do to that,

Being a thing immortal as itself?

It waves me forth again: I'll follow it.

HORATIO
What if it tempt you toward the flood, my lord,

Or to the dreadful summit of the cliff

That beetles o'er his base into the sea,

And there assume some other horrible form,

Which might deprive your sovereignty of reason

And draw you into madness? think of it:

The very place puts toys of desperation,

Without more motive, into every brain

That looks so many fathoms to the sea

And hears it roar beneath.

HAMLET
It waves me still.

Go on; I'll follow thee.

MARCELLUS
You shall not go, my lord.

HAMLET
Hold off your hands.

HORATIO
Be ruled; you shall not go.

HAMLET
My fate cries out,

And makes each petty artery in this body

As hardy as the Nemean lion's nerve.

Still am I call'd. Unhand me, gentlemen.

By heaven, I'll make a ghost of him that lets me!

I say, away! Go on; I'll follow thee.

Exeunt Ghost and HAMLET

HORATIO
He waxes desperate with imagination.

MARCELLUS
Let's follow; 'tis not fit thus to obey him.

HORATIO
Have after. To what issue will this come?

MARCELLUS
Something is rotten in the state of Denmark.

HORATIO
Heaven will direct it.

MARCELLUS
Nay, let's follow him.

Exeunt

NOTES

SCENE V. Another part of the platform.

Enter GHOST and HAMLET

HAMLET
Where wilt thou lead me? speak; I'll go no further.

Ghost
Mark me.

HAMLET
I will.

Ghost
My hour is almost come,

When I to sulphurous and tormenting flames

Must render up myself.

HAMLET
Alas, poor ghost!

Ghost
Pity me not, but lend thy serious hearing

To what I shall unfold.

HAMLET
Speak; I am bound to hear.

Ghost
So art thou to revenge, when thou shalt hear.

HAMLET
What?

Ghost
I am thy father's spirit,

Doom'd for a certain term to walk the night,

And for the day confined to fast in fires,

43

Till the foul crimes done in my days of nature

Are burnt and purged away. But that I am forbid

To tell the secrets of my prison-house,

I could a tale unfold whose lightest word

Would harrow up thy soul, freeze thy young blood,

Make thy two eyes, like stars, start from their spheres,

Thy knotted and combined locks to part

And each particular hair to stand on end,

Like quills upon the fretful porpentine:

But this eternal blazon must not be

To ears of flesh and blood. List, list, O, list!

If thou didst ever thy dear father love--

HAMLET
O God!

Ghost
Revenge his foul and most unnatural murder.

HAMLET
Murder!

Ghost
Murder most foul, as in the best it is;

But this most foul, strange and unnatural.

HAMLET
Haste me to know't, that I, with wings as swift

As meditation or the thoughts of love,

May sweep to my revenge.

Ghost
I find thee apt;

And duller shouldst thou be than the fat weed

That roots itself in ease on Lethe wharf,

Wouldst thou not stir in this. Now, Hamlet, hear:

'Tis given out that, sleeping in my orchard,

A serpent stung me; so the whole ear of Denmark

Is by a forged process of my death

Rankly abused: but know, thou noble youth,

The serpent that did sting thy father's life

Now wears his crown.

the serpent

-Cladius killed the king!

HAMLET
O my prophetic soul! My uncle!

Ghost
Ay, that incestuous, that adulterate beast,

With witchcraft of his wit, with traitorous gifts,--

O wicked wit and gifts, that have the power

So to seduce!--won to his shameful lust

The will of my most seeming-virtuous queen:

O Hamlet, what a falling-off was there!

From me, whose love was of that dignity

That it went hand in hand even with the vow

I made to her in marriage, and to decline

Upon a wretch whose natural gifts were poor

To those of mine!

But virtue, as it never will be moved,

Though lewdness court it in a shape of heaven,

So lust, though to a radiant angel link'd,

Will sate itself in a celestial bed,

And prey on garbage.

But, soft! methinks I scent the morning air;

Brief let me be. Sleeping within my orchard,

My custom always of the afternoon,

Upon my secure hour thy uncle stole,

With juice of cursed hebenon in a vial,

And in the porches of my ears did pour

The leperous distilment; whose effect

Holds such an enmity with blood of man

That swift as quicksilver it courses through

The natural gates and alleys of the body,

And with a sudden vigour doth posset

And curd, like eager droppings into milk,

The thin and wholesome blood: so did it mine;

And a most instant tetter bark'd about,

Most lazar-like, with vile and loathsome crust,

All my smooth body.

46

Thus was I, sleeping, by a brother's hand

Of life, of crown, of queen, at once dispatch'd:

Cut off even in the blossoms of my sin,

Unhousel'd, disappointed, unanel'd,

No reckoning made, but sent to my account

With all my imperfections on my head:

O, horrible! O, horrible! most horrible!

If thou hast nature in thee, bear it not;

Let not the royal bed of Denmark be

A couch for luxury and damned incest.

But, howsoever thou pursuest this act,

Taint not thy mind, nor let thy soul contrive

Against thy mother aught: leave her to heaven

And to those thorns that in her bosom lodge,

To prick and sting her. Fare thee well at once!

The glow-worm shows the matin to be near,

And 'gins to pale his uneffectual fire:

Adieu, adieu! Hamlet, remember me.

Exit

HAMLET
O all you host of heaven! O earth! what else?

And shall I couple hell? O, fie! Hold, hold, my heart;

And you, my sinews, grow not instant old,

But bear me stiffly up. Remember thee!

Ay, thou poor ghost, while memory holds a seat

In this distracted globe. Remember thee!

Yea, from the table of my memory

I'll wipe away all trivial fond records,

All saws of books, all forms, all pressures past,

That youth and observation copied there;

And thy commandment all alone shall live

Within the book and volume of my brain,

Unmix'd with baser matter: yes, by heaven!

O most pernicious woman!

O villain, villain, smiling, damned villain!

My tables,--meet it is I set it down,

That one may smile, and smile, and be a villain;

At least I'm sure it may be so in Denmark:

Writing
So, uncle, there you are. Now to my word;

It is 'Adieu, adieu! remember me.'

I have sworn 't.

MARCELLUS HORATIO
[Within] My lord, my lord,--

MARCELLUS
[Within] Lord Hamlet,--

HORATIO
[Within] Heaven secure him!

HAMLET
So be it!

HORATIO
[Within] Hillo, ho, ho, my lord!

HAMLET
Hillo, ho, ho, boy! come, bird, come.

Enter HORATIO and MARCELLUS

MARCELLUS
How is't, my noble lord?

HORATIO
What news, my lord?

HAMLET
O, wonderful!

HORATIO
Good my lord, tell it.

HAMLET
No; you'll reveal it.

HORATIO
Not I, my lord, by heaven.

MARCELLUS
Nor I, my lord.

HAMLET
How say you, then; would heart of man once think it?

But you'll be secret?

HORATIO MARCELLUS
Ay, by heaven, my lord.

HAMLET

There's ne'er a villain dwelling in all Denmark

But he's an arrant knave.

HORATIO

There needs no ghost, my lord, come from the grave

To tell us this.

HAMLET

Why, right; you are i' the right;

And so, without more circumstance at all,

I hold it fit that we shake hands and part:

You, as your business and desire shall point you;

For every man has business and desire,

Such as it is; and for mine own poor part,

Look you, I'll go pray.

HORATIO

These are but wild and whirling words, my lord.

HAMLET

I'm sorry they offend you, heartily;

Yes, 'faith heartily.

HORATIO

There's no offence, my lord.

HAMLET

Yes, by Saint Patrick, but there is, Horatio,

And much offence too. Touching this vision here,

It is an honest ghost, that let me tell you:

For your desire to know what is between us,

O'ermaster 't as you may. And now, good friends,

As you are friends, scholars and soldiers,

Give me one poor request.

HORATIO
What is't, my lord? we will.

HAMLET
Never make known what you have seen to-night.

HORATIO MARCELLUS
My lord, we will not.

HAMLET
Nay, but swear't.

HORATIO
In faith,

My lord, not I.

MARCELLUS
Nor I, my lord, in faith.

HAMLET
Upon my sword.

MARCELLUS
We have sworn, my lord, already.

HAMLET
Indeed, upon my sword, indeed.

Ghost
[Beneath] Swear.

HAMLET
Ah, ha, boy! say'st thou so? art thou there,

truepenny?

Come on--you hear this fellow in the cellarage--

Consent to swear.

HORATIO
Propose the oath, my lord.

HAMLET
Never to speak of this that you have seen,

Swear by my sword.

Ghost
[Beneath] Swear.

HAMLET
Hic et ubique? then we'll shift our ground.

Come hither, gentlemen,

And lay your hands again upon my sword:

Never to speak of this that you have heard,

Swear by my sword.

Ghost
[Beneath] Swear.

HAMLET
Well said, old mole! canst work i' the earth so fast?

A worthy pioner! Once more remove, good friends.

HORATIO
O day and night, but this is wondrous strange!

HAMLET
And therefore as a stranger give it welcome.

There are more things in heaven and earth, Horatio,

Than are dreamt of in your philosophy. But come;

HERE AND EVERYWHERE

Here, as before, never, so help you mercy,

How strange or odd soe'er I bear myself,

As I perchance hereafter shall think meet

To put an antic disposition on,

That you, at such times seeing me, never shall,

With arms encumber'd thus, or this headshake,

Or by pronouncing of some doubtful phrase,

As 'Well, well, we know,' or 'We could, an if we would,'

Or 'If we list to speak,' or 'There be, an if they might,'

Or such ambiguous giving out, to note

That you know aught of me: this not to do,

So grace and mercy at your most need help you, Swear.

Ghost
[Beneath] Swear.

HAMLET
Rest, rest, perturbed spirit!

They swear

So, gentlemen,

With all my love I do commend me to you:

And what so poor a man as Hamlet is

May do, to express his love and friending to you,

God willing, shall not lack. Let us go in together;

And still your fingers on your lips, I pray.

The time is out of joint: O cursed spite,

That ever I was born to set it right!

Nay, come, let's go together.

Exeunt

NOTES

NOTES

ACT II

SCENE I. A room in POLONIUS' house.

Enter POLONIUS and REYNALDO

LORD POLONIUS
Give him this money and these notes, Reynaldo.

REYNALDO
I will, my lord.

LORD POLONIUS
You shall do marvellous wisely, good Reynaldo,

Before you visit him, to make inquire

Of his behavior.

REYNALDO
My lord, I did intend it.

LORD POLONIUS
Marry, well said; very well said. Look you, sir,

Inquire me first what Danskers are in Paris;

And how, and who, what means, and where they keep,

What company, at what expense; and finding

By this encompassment and drift of question

That they do know my son, come you more nearer

Than your particular demands will touch it:

Take you, as 'twere, some distant knowledge of him;

As thus, 'I know his father and his friends,

And in part him: ' do you mark this, Reynaldo?

REYNALDO
Ay, very well, my lord.

LORD POLONIUS
'And in part him; but' you may say 'not well:

But, if't be he I mean, he's very wild;

Addicted so and so:' and there put on him

What forgeries you please; marry, none so rank

As may dishonour him; take heed of that;

But, sir, such wanton, wild and usual slips

As are companions noted and most known

To youth and liberty.

REYNALDO
As gaming, my lord.

LORD POLONIUS
Ay, or drinking, fencing, swearing, quarrelling,

Drabbing: you may go so far.

REYNALDO
My lord, that would dishonour him.

LORD POLONIUS
'Faith, no; as you may season it in the charge

You must not put another scandal on him,

That he is open to incontinency;

That's not my meaning: but breathe his faults so quaintly

That they may seem the taints of liberty,

The flash and outbreak of a fiery mind,

A savageness in unreclaimed blood,

Of general assault.

REYNALDO
But, my good lord,--

LORD POLONIUS
Wherefore should you do this?

REYNALDO
Ay, my lord,

I would know that.

LORD POLONIUS
Marry, sir, here's my drift;

And I believe, it is a fetch of wit:

You laying these slight sullies on my son,

As 'twere a thing a little soil'd i' the working, Mark you,

Your party in converse, him you would sound,

Having ever seen in the prenominate crimes

The youth you breathe of guilty, be assured

He closes with you in this consequence;

'Good sir,' or so, or 'friend,' or 'gentleman,'

According to the phrase or the addition

Of man and country.

REYNALDO
Very good, my lord.

LORD POLONIUS
And then, sir, does he this--he does--what was I

about to say? By the mass, I was about to say

something: where did I leave?

REYNALDO
At 'closes in the consequence,' at 'friend or so,'

and 'gentleman.'

LORD POLONIUS
At 'closes in the consequence,' ay, marry;

He closes thus: 'I know the gentleman;

I saw him yesterday, or t' other day,

Or then, or then; with such, or such; and, as you say,

There was a' gaming; there o'ertook in's rouse;

There falling out at tennis:' or perchance,

'I saw him enter such a house of sale,'

Videlicet, a brothel, or so forth.

See you now;

Your bait of falsehood takes this carp of truth:

And thus do we of wisdom and of reach,

With windlasses and with assays of bias,

By indirections find directions out:

So by my former lecture and advice,

Shall you my son. You have me, have you not?

REYNALDO
My lord, I have.

LORD POLONIUS

God be wi' you; fare you well.

REYNALDO

Good my lord!

LORD POLONIUS

Observe his inclination in yourself.

REYNALDO

I shall, my lord.

LORD POLONIUS

And let him ply his music.

REYNALDO

Well, my lord.

LORD POLONIUS

Farewell!

Exit REYNALDO

Enter OPHELIA

How now, Ophelia! what's the matter?

OPHELIA

O, my lord, my lord, I have been so affrighted!

LORD POLONIUS

With what, i' the name of God?

OPHELIA

My lord, as I was sewing in my closet,

Lord Hamlet, with his doublet all unbraced;

No hat upon his head; his stockings foul'd,

Ungarter'd, and down-gyved to his ancle;

Pale as his shirt; his knees knocking each other;

And with a look so piteous in purport

As if he had been loosed out of hell

To speak of horrors,--he comes before me.

LORD POLONIUS
Mad for thy love?

OPHELIA
My lord, I do not know;

But truly, I do fear it.

LORD POLONIUS
What said he?

OPHELIA
He took me by the wrist and held me hard;

Then goes he to the length of all his arm;

And, with his other hand thus o'er his brow,

He falls to such perusal of my face

As he would draw it. Long stay'd he so;

At last, a little shaking of mine arm

And thrice his head thus waving up and down,

He raised a sigh so piteous and profound

As it did seem to shatter all his bulk

And end his being: that done, he lets me go:

And, with his head over his shoulder turn'd,

He seem'd to find his way without his eyes;

For out o' doors he went without their helps,

And, to the last, bended their light on me.

LORD POLONIUS
Come, go with me: I will go seek the king.

This is the very ecstasy of love,

Whose violent property fordoes itself

And leads the will to desperate undertakings

As oft as any passion under heaven

That does afflict our natures. I am sorry.

What, have you given him any hard words of late?

OPHELIA
No, my good lord, but, as you did command,

I did repel his fetters and denied

His access to me.

LORD POLONIUS
That hath made him mad.

I am sorry that with better heed and judgment

I had not quoted him: I fear'd he did but trifle,

And meant to wreck thee; but, beshrew my jealousy!

By heaven, it is as proper to our age

To cast beyond ourselves in our opinions

As it is common for the younger sort

To lack discretion. Come, go we to the king:

This must be known; which, being kept close, might
move
More grief to hide than hate to utter love.

Exeunt

SCENE II. A room in the castle.

Enter KING CLAUDIUS, QUEEN GERTRUDE, ROSENCRANTZ,

GUILDENSTERN, and Attendants

KING CLAUDIUS
Welcome, dear Rosencrantz and Guildenstern!

Moreover that we much did long to see you,

The need we have to use you did provoke

Our hasty sending. Something have you heard

Of Hamlet's transformation; so call it,

Sith nor the exterior nor the inward man

Resembles that it was. What it should be,

More than his father's death, that thus hath put him

So much from the understanding of himself,

I cannot dream of: I entreat you both,

That, being of so young days brought up with him,

And sith so neighbour'd to his youth and havior,

That you vouchsafe your rest here in our court

Some little time: so by your companies

To draw him on to pleasures, and to gather,

So much as from occasion you may glean,

Whether aught, to us unknown, afflicts him thus,

That, open'd, lies within our remedy.

QUEEN GERTRUDE
Good gentlemen, he hath much talk'd of you;

And sure I am two men there are not living

To whom he more adheres. If it will please you

To show us so much gentry and good will

As to expend your time with us awhile,

For the supply and profit of our hope,

Your visitation shall receive such thanks

As fits a king's remembrance.

ROSENCRANTZ
Both your majesties

Might, by the sovereign power you have of us,

Put your dread pleasures more into command

Than to entreaty.

GUILDENSTERN
But we both obey,

And here give up ourselves, in the full bent

To lay our service freely at your feet,

To be commanded.

KING CLAUDIUS
Thanks, Rosencrantz and gentle Guildenstern.

QUEEN GERTRUDE
Thanks, Guildenstern and gentle Rosencrantz:

And I beseech you instantly to visit

My too much changed son. Go, some of you,

And bring these gentlemen where Hamlet is.

GUILDENSTERN
Heavens make our presence and our practises

Pleasant and helpful to him!

QUEEN GERTRUDE
Ay, amen!

Exeunt ROSENCRANTZ, GUILDENSTERN, and some Attendants

Enter POLONIUS

LORD POLONIUS
The ambassadors from Norway, my good lord,

Are joyfully return'd.

KING CLAUDIUS
Thou still hast been the father of good news.

LORD POLONIUS
Have I, my lord? I assure my good liege,

I hold my duty, as I hold my soul,

Both to my God and to my gracious king:

And I do think, or else this brain of mine

Hunts not the trail of policy so sure

As it hath used to do, that I have found

The very cause of Hamlet's lunacy.

KING CLAUDIUS
O, speak of that; that do I long to hear.

LORD POLONIUS
Give first admittance to the ambassadors;

My news shall be the fruit to that great feast.

KING CLAUDIUS
Thyself do grace to them, and bring them in.

Exit POLONIUS

He tells me, my dear Gertrude, he hath found

The head and source of all your son's distemper.

QUEEN GERTRUDE
I doubt it is no other but the main;

His father's death, and our o'erhasty marriage.

KING CLAUDIUS
Well, we shall sift him.

Re-enter POLONIUS, with VOLTIMAND and CORNELIUS

Welcome, my good friends!

Say, Voltimand, what from our brother Norway?

VOLTIMAND
Most fair return of greetings and desires.

Upon our first, he sent out to suppress

His nephew's levies; which to him appear'd

To be a preparation 'gainst the Polack;

But, better look'd into, he truly found

It was against your highness: whereat grieved,

That so his sickness, age and impotence

Was falsely borne in hand, sends out arrests

On Fortinbras; which he, in brief, obeys;

Receives rebuke from Norway, and in fine

Makes vow before his uncle never more

To give the assay of arms against your majesty.

Whereon old Norway, overcome with joy,

Gives him three thousand crowns in annual fee,

And his commission to employ those soldiers,

So levied as before, against the Polack:

With an entreaty, herein further shown,

Giving a paper

That it might please you to give quiet pass

Through your dominions for this enterprise,

On such regards of safety and allowance

As therein are set down.

KING CLAUDIUS
It likes us well;

And at our more consider'd time well read,

Answer, and think upon this business.

Meantime we thank you for your well-took labour:

Go to your rest; at night we'll feast together:

Most welcome home!

Exeunt VOLTIMAND and CORNELIUS

LORD POLONIUS
This business is well ended.

My liege, and madam, to expostulate

What majesty should be, what duty is,

Why day is day, night night, and time is time,

Were nothing but to waste night, day and time.

Therefore, since brevity is the soul of wit,

And tediousness the limbs and outward flourishes,

I will be brief: your noble son is mad:

Mad call I it; for, to define true madness,

What is't but to be nothing else but mad?

But let that go.

QUEEN GERTRUDE
More matter, with less art.

LORD POLONIUS
Madam, I swear I use no art at all.

That he is mad, 'tis true: 'tis true 'tis pity;

And pity 'tis 'tis true: a foolish figure;

But farewell it, for I will use no art.

Mad let us grant him, then: and now remains

That we find out the cause of this effect,

Or rather say, the cause of this defect,

For this effect defective comes by cause:

Thus it remains, and the remainder thus. Perpend.

I have a daughter--have while she is mine--

Who, in her duty and obedience, mark,

Hath given me this: now gather, and surmise.

Reads

'To the celestial and my soul's idol, the most

beautified Ophelia,'--

That's an ill phrase, a vile phrase; 'beautified' is

a vile phrase: but you shall hear. Thus:

Reads

'In her excellent white bosom, these, & c.'

QUEEN GERTRUDE
Came this from Hamlet to her?

LORD POLONIUS
Good madam, stay awhile; I will be faithful.

Reads

'Doubt thou the stars are fire;

Doubt that the sun doth move;

Doubt truth to be a liar;

But never doubt I love.

'O dear Ophelia, I am ill at these numbers;

I have not art to reckon my groans: but that

I love thee best, O most best, believe it. Adieu.

'Thine evermore most dear lady, whilst

this machine is to him, HAMLET.'

This, in obedience, hath my daughter shown me,

And more above, hath his solicitings,

As they fell out by time, by means and place,

All given to mine ear.

KING CLAUDIUS
But how hath she

Received his love?

LORD POLONIUS
What do you think of me?

KING CLAUDIUS
As of a man faithful and honourable.

LORD POLONIUS
I would fain prove so. But what might you think,

When I had seen this hot love on the wing--

As I perceived it, I must tell you that,

Before my daughter told me--what might you,

Or my dear majesty your queen here, think,

If I had play'd the desk or table-book,

Or given my heart a winking, mute and dumb,

Or look'd upon this love with idle sight;

What might you think? No, I went round to work,

And my young mistress thus I did bespeak:

'Lord Hamlet is a prince, out of thy star;

This must not be:' and then I precepts gave her,

That she should lock herself from his resort,

Admit no messengers, receive no tokens.

Which done, she took the fruits of my advice;

And he, repulsed--a short tale to make--

Fell into a sadness, then into a fast,

Thence to a watch, thence into a weakness,

Thence to a lightness, and, by this declension,

Into the madness wherein now he raves,

And all we mourn for.

KING CLAUDIUS
Do you think 'tis this?

QUEEN GERTRUDE
It may be, very likely.

LORD POLONIUS
Hath there been such a time--I'd fain know that--

That I have positively said 'Tis so,'

When it proved otherwise?

KING CLAUDIUS
Not that I know.

LORD POLONIUS
[Pointing to his head and shoulder]

Take this from this, if this be otherwise:

If circumstances lead me, I will find

Where truth is hid, though it were hid indeed

Within the centre.

KING CLAUDIUS
How may we try it further?

LORD POLONIUS
You know, sometimes he walks four hours together

Here in the lobby.

QUEEN GERTRUDE
So he does indeed.

LORD POLONIUS
At such a time I'll loose my daughter to him:

Be you and I behind an arras then;

Mark the encounter: if he love her not

And be not from his reason fall'n thereon,

Let me be no assistant for a state,

But keep a farm and carters.

KING CLAUDIUS
We will try it.

QUEEN GERTRUDE
But, look, where sadly the poor wretch comes reading.

LORD POLONIUS
Away, I do beseech you, both away:

I'll board him presently.

Exeunt KING CLAUDIUS, QUEEN GERTRUDE, and Attendants
Enter HAMLET, reading
O, give me leave:

How does my good Lord Hamlet?

HAMLET
Well, God-a-mercy.

LORD POLONIUS
Do you know me, my lord?

HAMLET

Excellent well; you are a fishmonger.

LORD POLONIUS

Not I, my lord.

HAMLET

Then I would you were so honest a man.

LORD POLONIUS

Honest, my lord!

HAMLET

Ay, sir; to be honest, as this world goes, is to be

one man picked out of ten thousand.

LORD POLONIUS

That's very true, my lord.

HAMLET

For if the sun breed maggots in a dead dog, being a

god kissing carrion,--Have you a daughter?

LORD POLONIUS

I have, my lord.

HAMLET

Let her not walk i' the sun: conception is a

blessing: but not as your daughter may conceive.

Friend, look to 't.

LORD POLONIUS

[Aside] How say you by that? Still harping on my

daughter: yet he knew me not at first; he said I

was a fishmonger: he is far gone, far gone: and

truly in my youth I suffered much extremity for

love; very near this. I'll speak to him again.

What do you read, my lord?

HAMLET
Words, words, words.

LORD POLONIUS
What is the matter, my lord?

HAMLET
Between who?

LORD POLONIUS
I mean, the matter that you read, my lord.

HAMLET
Slanders, sir: for the satirical rogue says here

that old men have grey beards, that their faces are

wrinkled, their eyes purging thick amber and

plum-tree gum and that they have a plentiful lack of

wit, together with most weak hams: all which, sir,

though I most powerfully and potently believe, yet

I hold it not honesty to have it thus set down, for

yourself, sir, should be old as I am, if like a crab

you could go backward.

LORD POLONIUS
[Aside] Though this be madness, yet there is method

in 't. Will you walk out of the air, my lord?

HAMLET
Into my grave.

LORD POLONIUS

Indeed, that is out o' the air.

Aside

How pregnant sometimes his replies are! a happiness

that often madness hits on, which reason and sanity

could not so prosperously be delivered of. I will

leave him, and suddenly contrive the means of

meeting between him and my daughter.--My honourable

lord, I will most humbly take my leave of you.

HAMLET
You cannot, sir, take from me any thing that I will

more willingly part withal: except my life, except

my life, except my life.

LORD POLONIUS
Fare you well, my lord.

HAMLET
These tedious old fools!

Enter ROSENCRANTZ and GUILDENSTERN

LORD POLONIUS
You go to seek the Lord Hamlet; there he is.

ROSENCRANTZ
[To POLONIUS] God save you, sir!

Exit POLONIUS

GUILDENSTERN
My honoured lord!

ROSENCRANTZ
My most dear lord!

HAMLET

My excellent good friends! How dost thou,

Guildenstern? Ah, Rosencrantz! Good lads, how do ye both?

ROSENCRANTZ

As the indifferent children of the earth.

GUILDENSTERN

Happy, in that we are not over-happy;

On fortune's cap we are not the very button.

HAMLET

Nor the soles of her shoe?

ROSENCRANTZ

Neither, my lord.

HAMLET

Then you live about her waist, or in the middle of

her favours?

GUILDENSTERN

'Faith, her privates we.

HAMLET

In the secret parts of fortune? O, most true; she

is a strumpet. What's the news?

ROSENCRANTZ

None, my lord, but that the world's grown honest.

HAMLET

Then is doomsday near: but your news is not true.

Let me question more in particular: what have you,

my good friends, deserved at the hands of fortune,

that she sends you to prison hither?

GUILDENSTERN
Prison, my lord!

HAMLET
Denmark's a prison.

ROSENCRANTZ
Then is the world one.

HAMLET
A goodly one; in which there are many confines,

wards and dungeons, Denmark being one o' the worst.

ROSENCRANTZ
We think not so, my lord.

HAMLET
Why, then, 'tis none to you; for there is nothing

either good or bad, but thinking makes it so: to me

it is a prison.

ROSENCRANTZ
Why then, your ambition makes it one; 'tis too

narrow for your mind.

HAMLET
O God, I could be bounded in a nut shell and count

myself a king of infinite space, were it not that I

have bad dreams.

GUILDENSTERN
Which dreams indeed are ambition, for the very

substance of the ambitious is merely the shadow of a dream.

HAMLET
A dream itself is but a shadow.

ROSENCRANTZ

Truly, and I hold ambition of so airy and light a

quality that it is but a shadow's shadow.

HAMLET

Then are our beggars bodies, and our monarchs and

outstretched heroes the beggars' shadows. Shall we

to the court? for, by my fay, I cannot reason.

ROSENCRANTZ GUILDENSTERN

We'll wait upon you.

HAMLET

No such matter: I will not sort you with the rest

of my servants, for, to speak to you like an honest

man, I am most dreadfully attended. But, in the

beaten way of friendship, what make you at Elsinore?

ROSENCRANTZ

To visit you, my lord; no other occasion.

HAMLET

Beggar that I am, I am even poor in thanks; but I

thank you: and sure, dear friends, my thanks are

too dear a halfpenny. Were you not sent for? Is it

your own inclining? Is it a free visitation? Come,

deal justly with me: come, come; nay, speak.

GUILDENSTERN

What should we say, my lord?

HAMLET

Why, any thing, but to the purpose. You were sent

for; and there is a kind of confession in your looks

which your modesties have not craft enough to colour:

I know the good king and queen have sent for you.

ROSENCRANTZ
To what end, my lord?

HAMLET
That you must teach me. But let me conjure you, by

the rights of our fellowship, by the consonancy of

our youth, by the obligation of our ever-preserved

love, and by what more dear a better proposer could

charge you withal, be even and direct with me,

whether you were sent for, or no?

ROSENCRANTZ
[Aside to GUILDENSTERN] What say you?

HAMLET
[Aside] Nay, then, I have an eye of you.--If you

love me, hold not off.

GUILDENSTERN
My lord, we were sent for.

HAMLET
I will tell you why; so shall my anticipation

prevent your discovery, and your secrecy to the king

and queen moult no feather. I have of late--but

wherefore I know not--lost all my mirth, forgone all

custom of exercises; and indeed it goes so heavily

with my disposition that this goodly frame, the

earth, seems to me a sterile promontory, this most

excellent canopy, the air, look you, this brave

o'erhanging firmament, this majestical roof fretted

with golden fire, why, it appears no other thing to

me than a foul and pestilent congregation of vapours.

What a piece of work is a man! how noble in reason!

how infinite in faculty! in form and moving how

express and admirable! in action how like an angel!

in apprehension how like a god! the beauty of the

world! the paragon of animals! And yet, to me,

what is this quintessence of dust? man delights not

me: no, nor woman neither, though by your smiling

you seem to say so.

ROSENCRANTZ
My lord, there was no such stuff in my thoughts.

HAMLET
Why did you laugh then, when I said 'man delights not me'?

ROSENCRANTZ
To think, my lord, if you delight not in man, what

lenten entertainment the players shall receive from

you: we coted them on the way; and hither are they

coming, to offer you service.

HAMLET
He that plays the king shall be welcome; his majesty

shall have tribute of me; the adventurous knight

shall use his foil and target; the lover shall not

sigh gratis; the humourous man shall end his part

in peace; the clown shall make those laugh whose

lungs are tickled o' the sere; and the lady shall

say her mind freely, or the blank verse shall halt

for't. What players are they?

ROSENCRANTZ
Even those you were wont to take delight in, the

tragedians of the city.

HAMLET
How chances it they travel? their residence, both

in reputation and profit, was better both ways.

ROSENCRANTZ
I think their inhibition comes by the means of the

late innovation.

HAMLET
Do they hold the same estimation they did when I was

in the city? are they so followed?

ROSENCRANTZ
No, indeed, are they not.

HAMLET
How comes it? do they grow rusty?

ROSENCRANTZ
Nay, their endeavour keeps in the wonted pace: but

there is, sir, an aery of children, little eyases,

that cry out on the top of question, and are most

tyrannically clapped for't: these are now the

fashion, and so berattle the common stages--so they

call them--that many wearing rapiers are afraid of

goose-quills and dare scarce come thither.

HAMLET
What, are they children? who maintains 'em? how are

they escoted? Will they pursue the quality no

longer than they can sing? will they not say

afterwards, if they should grow themselves to common

players--as it is most like, if their means are no

better--their writers do them wrong, to make them

exclaim against their own succession?

ROSENCRANTZ
'Faith, there has been much to do on both sides; and

the nation holds it no sin to tarre them to

controversy: there was, for a while, no money bid

for argument, unless the poet and the player went to

cuffs in the question.

HAMLET
Is't possible?

GUILDENSTERN
O, there has been much throwing about of brains.

HAMLET
Do the boys carry it away?

ROSENCRANTZ
Ay, that they do, my lord; Hercules and his load too.

HAMLET
It is not very strange; for mine uncle is king of

Denmark, and those that would make mows at him while

my father lived, give twenty, forty, fifty, an

hundred ducats a-piece for his picture in little.

'Sblood, there is something in this more than

natural, if philosophy could find it out.

Flourish of trumpets within

GUILDENSTERN
There are the players.

HAMLET
Gentlemen, you are welcome to Elsinore. Your hands,

come then: the appurtenance of welcome is fashion

and ceremony: let me comply with you in this garb,

lest my extent to the players, which, I tell you,

must show fairly outward, should more appear like

entertainment than yours. You are welcome: but my

uncle-father and aunt-mother are deceived.

GUILDENSTERN
In what, my dear lord?

HAMLET

I am but mad north-north-west: when the wind is

southerly I know a hawk from a handsaw.

Enter POLONIUS

LORD POLONIUS

Well be with you, gentlemen!

HAMLET

Hark you, Guildenstern; and you too: at each ear a

hearer: that great baby you see there is not yet

out of his swaddling-clouts.

ROSENCRANTZ

Happily he's the second time come to them; for they

say an old man is twice a child.

HAMLET

I will prophesy he comes to tell me of the players;

mark it. You say right, sir: o' Monday morning;

'twas so indeed.

LORD POLONIUS

My lord, I have news to tell you.

HAMLET

My lord, I have news to tell you.

When Roscius was an actor in Rome,--

LORD POLONIUS

The actors are come hither, my lord.

HAMLET

Buz, buz!

LORD POLONIUS
Upon mine honour,--

HAMLET
Then came each actor on his ass,--

LORD POLONIUS
The best actors in the world, either for tragedy,

comedy, history, pastoral, pastoral-comical,

historical-pastoral, tragical-historical, tragical-

comical-historical-pastoral, scene individable, or

poem unlimited: Seneca cannot be too heavy, nor

Plautus too light. For the law of writ and the

liberty, these are the only men.

HAMLET
O Jephthah, judge of Israel, what a treasure hadst thou!

LORD POLONIUS
What a treasure had he, my lord?

HAMLET
Why,

'One fair daughter and no more,

The which he loved passing well.'

LORD POLONIUS
[Aside] Still on my daughter.

HAMLET
Am I not i' the right, old Jephthah?

LORD POLONIUS
If you call me Jephthah, my lord, I have a daughter

that I love passing well.

HAMLET

Nay, that follows not.

LORD POLONIUS

What follows, then, my lord?

HAMLET

Why,

'As by lot, God wot,'

and then, you know,

'It came to pass, as most like it was,'--

the first row of the pious chanson will show you

more; for look, where my abridgement comes.

Enter four or five Players

You are welcome, masters; welcome, all. I am glad

to see thee well. Welcome, good friends. O, my old

friend! thy face is valenced since I saw thee last:

comest thou to beard me in Denmark? What, my young

lady and mistress! By'r lady, your ladyship is

nearer to heaven than when I saw you last, by the

altitude of a chopine. Pray God, your voice, like

apiece of uncurrent gold, be not cracked within the

ring. Masters, you are all welcome. We'll e'en

to't like French falconers, fly at any thing we see:

we'll have a speech straight: come, give us a taste

of your quality; come, a passionate speech.

First Player
What speech, my lord?

HAMLET
I heard thee speak me a speech once, but it was

never acted; or, if it was, not above once; for the

play, I remember, pleased not the million; 'twas

caviare to the general: but it was--as I received

it, and others, whose judgments in such matters

cried in the top of mine--an excellent play, well

digested in the scenes, set down with as much

modesty as cunning. I remember, one said there

were no sallets in the lines to make the matter

savoury, nor no matter in the phrase that might

indict the author of affectation; but called it an

honest method, as wholesome as sweet, and by very

much more handsome than fine. One speech in it I

chiefly loved: 'twas Aeneas' tale to Dido; and

thereabout of it especially, where he speaks of

Priam's slaughter: if it live in your memory, begin

at this line: let me see, let me see--

'The rugged Pyrrhus, like the Hyrcanian beast,'--

it is not so:--it begins with Pyrrhus:--

'The rugged Pyrrhus, he whose sable arms,

Black as his purpose, did the night resemble

When he lay couched in the ominous horse,

Hath now this dread and black complexion smear'd

With heraldry more dismal; head to foot

Now is he total gules; horridly trick'd

With blood of fathers, mothers, daughters, sons,

Baked and impasted with the parching streets,

That lend a tyrannous and damned light

To their lord's murder: roasted in wrath and fire,

And thus o'er-sized with coagulate gore,

With eyes like carbuncles, the hellish Pyrrhus

Old grandsire Priam seeks.'

So, proceed you.

LORD POLONIUS
'Fore God, my lord, well spoken, with good accent and

good discretion.

First Player
'Anon he finds him

Striking too short at Greeks; his antique sword,

Rebellious to his arm, lies where it falls,

Repugnant to command: unequal match'd,

Pyrrhus at Priam drives; in rage strikes wide;

But with the whiff and wind of his fell sword

The unnerved father falls. Then senseless Ilium,

Seeming to feel this blow, with flaming top

Stoops to his base, and with a hideous crash

Takes prisoner Pyrrhus' ear: for, lo! his sword,

Which was declining on the milky head

Of reverend Priam, seem'd i' the air to stick:

So, as a painted tyrant, Pyrrhus stood,

And like a neutral to his will and matter,

Did nothing.

But, as we often see, against some storm,

A silence in the heavens, the rack stand still,

The bold winds speechless and the orb below

As hush as death, anon the dreadful thunder

Doth rend the region, so, after Pyrrhus' pause,

Aroused vengeance sets him new a-work;

And never did the Cyclops' hammers fall

On Mars's armour forged for proof eterne

With less remorse than Pyrrhus' bleeding sword

Now falls on Priam.

Out, out, thou strumpet, Fortune! All you gods,

In general synod 'take away her power;

Break all the spokes and fellies from her wheel,

And bowl the round nave down the hill of heaven,

As low as to the fiends!'

LORD POLONIUS
This is too long.

HAMLET
It shall to the barber's, with your beard. Prithee,

say on: he's for a jig or a tale of bawdry, or he

sleeps: say on: come to Hecuba.

First Player
'But who, O, who had seen the mobled queen--'

HAMLET
'The mobled queen?'

LORD POLONIUS
That's good; 'mobled queen' is good.

First Player
'Run barefoot up and down, threatening the flames

With bisson rheum; a clout upon that head

Where late the diadem stood, and for a robe,

About her lank and all o'er-teemed loins,

A blanket, in the alarm of fear caught up;

Who this had seen, with tongue in venom steep'd,

'Gainst Fortune's state would treason have

pronounced:

But if the gods themselves did see her then

When she saw Pyrrhus make malicious sport

In mincing with his sword her husband's limbs,

The instant burst of clamour that she made,

Unless things mortal move them not at all,

Would have made milch the burning eyes of heaven,

And passion in the gods.'

LORD POLONIUS
Look, whether he has not turned his colour and has

tears in's eyes. Pray you, no more.

HAMLET
'Tis well: I'll have thee speak out the rest soon.

Good my lord, will you see the players well

bestowed? Do you hear, let them be well used; for

they are the abstract and brief chronicles of the

time: after your death you were better have a bad

epitaph than their ill report while you live.

LORD POLONIUS
My lord, I will use them according to their desert.

HAMLET
God's bodykins, man, much better: use every man

after his desert, and who should 'scape whipping?

Use them after your own honour and dignity: the less

they deserve, the more merit is in your bounty.

Take them in.

LORD POLONIUS
Come, sirs.

HAMLET
Follow him, friends: we'll hear a play to-morrow.

Exit POLONIUS with all the Players but the First

Dost thou hear me, old friend; can you play the

Murder of Gonzago?

First Player
Ay, my lord.

HAMLET
We'll ha't to-morrow night. You could, for a need,

study a speech of some dozen or sixteen lines, which

I would set down and insert in't, could you not?

First Player
Ay, my lord.

HAMLET
Very well. Follow that lord; and look you mock him

not.

Exit First Player
My good friends, I'll leave you till night: you are

welcome to Elsinore.

ROSENCRANTZ
Good my lord!

HAMLET
Ay, so, God be wi' ye;

Exeunt ROSENCRANTZ and GUILDENSTERN
Now I am alone.

O, what a rogue and peasant slave am I!

Is it not monstrous that this player here,

But in a fiction, in a dream of passion,

Could force his soul so to his own conceit

That from her working all his visage wann'd,

Tears in his eyes, distraction in's aspect,

A broken voice, and his whole function suiting

With forms to his conceit? and all for nothing!

For Hecuba!

What's Hecuba to him, or he to Hecuba,

That he should weep for her? What would he do,

Had he the motive and the cue for passion

That I have? He would drown the stage with tears

And cleave the general ear with horrid speech,

Make mad the guilty and appal the free,

Confound the ignorant, and amaze indeed

The very faculties of eyes and ears. Yet I,

A dull and muddy-mettled rascal, peak,

Like John-a-dreams, unpregnant of my cause,

And can say nothing; no, not for a king,

Upon whose property and most dear life

A damn'd defeat was made. Am I a coward?

Who calls me villain? breaks my pate across?

Plucks off my beard, and blows it in my face?

Tweaks me by the nose? gives me the lie i' the throat,

As deep as to the lungs? who does me this?

Ha!

'Swounds, I should take it: for it cannot be

But I am pigeon-liver'd and lack gall

To make oppression bitter, or ere this

I should have fatted all the region kites

With this slave's offal: bloody, bawdy villain!

Remorseless, treacherous, lecherous, kindless villain!

O, vengeance!

Why, what an ass am I! This is most brave,

That I, the son of a dear father murder'd,

Prompted to my revenge by heaven and hell,

Must, like a whore, unpack my heart with words,

And fall a-cursing, like a very drab,

A scullion!

Fie upon't! foh! About, my brain! I have heard

That guilty creatures sitting at a play

Have by the very cunning of the scene

Been struck so to the soul that presently

They have proclaim'd their malefactions;

For murder, though it have no tongue, will speak

With most miraculous organ. I'll have these players

Play something like the murder of my father

Before mine uncle: I'll observe his looks;

I'll tent him to the quick: if he but blench,

I know my course. The spirit that I have seen

May be the devil: and the devil hath power

To assume a pleasing shape; yea, and perhaps

Out of my weakness and my melancholy,

As he is very potent with such spirits,

Abuses me to damn me: I'll have grounds

More relative than this: the play 's the thing

Wherein I'll catch the conscience of the king.

Exit

NOTES

NOTES

NOTES

ACT III

SCENE I. A room in the castle.

Enter KING CLAUDIUS, QUEEN GERTRUDE, POLONIUS, OPHELIA, ROSENCRANTZ, and GUILDENSTERN

KING CLAUDIUS
And can you, by no drift of circumstance,

Get from him why he puts on this confusion,

Grating so harshly all his days of quiet

With turbulent and dangerous lunacy?

ROSENCRANTZ
He does confess he feels himself distracted;

But from what cause he will by no means speak.

GUILDENSTERN
Nor do we find him forward to be sounded,

But, with a crafty madness, keeps aloof,

When we would bring him on to some confession

Of his true state.

QUEEN GERTRUDE
Did he receive you well?

ROSENCRANTZ
Most like a gentleman.

GUILDENSTERN
But with much forcing of his disposition.

ROSENCRANTZ
Niggard of question; but, of our demands,

Most free in his reply.

QUEEN GERTRUDE
Did you assay him?

To any pastime?

ROSENCRANTZ
Madam, it so fell out, that certain players

We o'er-raught on the way: of these we told him;

And there did seem in him a kind of joy

To hear of it: they are about the court,

And, as I think, they have already order

This night to play before him.

LORD POLONIUS
'Tis most true:

And he beseech'd me to entreat your majesties

To hear and see the matter.

KING CLAUDIUS
With all my heart; and it doth much content me

To hear him so inclined.

Good gentlemen, give him a further edge,

And drive his purpose on to these delights.

ROSENCRANTZ
We shall, my lord.

Exeunt ROSENCRANTZ and GUILDENSTERN

KING CLAUDIUS
Sweet Gertrude, leave us too;

For we have closely sent for Hamlet hither,

That he, as 'twere by accident, may here

Affront Ophelia:

Her father and myself, lawful espials,

Will so bestow ourselves that, seeing, unseen,

We may of their encounter frankly judge,

And gather by him, as he is behaved,

If 't be the affliction of his love or no

That thus he suffers for.

QUEEN GERTRUDE
I shall obey you.

And for your part, Ophelia, I do wish

That your good beauties be the happy cause

Of Hamlet's wildness: so shall I hope your virtues

Will bring him to his wonted way again,

To both your honours.

OPHELIA
Madam, I wish it may.

Exit QUEEN GERTRUDE

LORD POLONIUS
Ophelia, walk you here. Gracious, so please you,

We will bestow ourselves.

To OPHELIA
Read on this book;

That show of such an exercise may colour

Your loneliness. We are oft to blame in this,--

'Tis too much proved--that with devotion's visage

And pious action we do sugar o'er

The devil himself.

KING CLAUDIUS
[Aside] O, 'tis too true!

How smart a lash that speech doth give my conscience!

The harlot's cheek, beautied with plastering art,

Is not more ugly to the thing that helps it

Than is my deed to my most painted word:

O heavy burthen!

LORD POLONIUS
I hear him coming: let's withdraw, my lord.

Exeunt KING CLAUDIUS and POLONIUS

Enter HAMLET

HAMLET
To be, or not to be, that is the question,

Whether 'tis nobler in the mind to suffer

The slings and arrows of outrageous fortune,

Or to take arms against a sea of troubles,

And by opposing end them? To die: to sleep;

No more; and by a sleep to say we end

The heart-ache and the thousand natural shocks

That flesh is heir to, 'tis a consummation

Devoutly to be wish'd. To die, to sleep;

To sleep: perchance to dream: ay, there's the rub;

For in that sleep of death what dreams may come

When we have shuffled off this mortal coil,

Must give us pause: there's the respect

That makes calamity of so long life;

For who would bear the whips and scorns of time,

The oppressor's wrong, the proud man's contumely,

The pangs of despised love, the law's delay,

The insolence of office and the spurns

That patient merit of the unworthy takes,

When he himself might his quietus make

With a bare bodkin? who would fardels bear,

To grunt and sweat under a weary life,

But that the dread of something after death,

The undiscover'd country from whose bourn

No traveller returns, puzzles the will

And makes us rather bear those ills we have

Than fly to others that we know not of?

Thus conscience does make cowards of us all;

And thus the native hue of resolution

Is sicklied o'er with the pale cast of thought,

And enterprises of great pith and moment

With this regard their currents turn awry,

And lose the name of action.--Soft you now!

The fair Ophelia! Nymph, in thy orisons

Be all my sins remember'd.

OPHELIA
Good my lord,

How does your honour for this many a day?

HAMLET
I humbly thank you; well, well, well.

OPHELIA
My lord, I have remembrances of yours,

That I have longed long to re-deliver;

I pray you, now receive them.

HAMLET
No, not I;

I never gave you aught.

OPHELIA
My honour'd lord, you know right well you did;

And, with them, words of so sweet breath composed

As made the things more rich: their perfume lost,

Take these again; for to the noble mind

Rich gifts wax poor when givers prove unkind.

There, my lord.

HAMLET
Ha, ha! are you honest?

OPHELIA
My lord?

HAMLET
Are you fair?

OPHELIA
What means your lordship?

HAMLET
That if you be honest and fair, your honesty should

admit no discourse to your beauty.

OPHELIA
Could beauty, my lord, have better commerce than

with honesty?

HAMLET
Ay, truly; for the power of beauty will sooner

transform honesty from what it is to a bawd than the

force of honesty can translate beauty into his

likeness: this was sometime a paradox, but now the

time gives it proof. I did love you once.

OPHELIA
Indeed, my lord, you made me believe so.

HAMLET
You should not have believed me; for virtue cannot

so inoculate our old stock but we shall relish of

it: I loved you not.

OPHELIA
I was the more deceived.

HAMLET
Get thee to a nunnery: why wouldst thou be a

breeder of sinners? I am myself indifferent honest;

but yet I could accuse me of such things that it

were better my mother had not borne me: I am very

proud, revengeful, ambitious, with more offences at

my beck than I have thoughts to put them in,

imagination to give them shape, or time to act them

in. What should such fellows as I do crawling

between earth and heaven? We are arrant knaves,

all; believe none of us. Go thy ways to a nunnery.

Where's your father?

OPHELIA
At home, my lord.

HAMLET
Let the doors be shut upon him, that he may play the

fool no where but in's own house. Farewell.

OPHELIA
O, help him, you sweet heavens!

HAMLET
If thou dost marry, I'll give thee this plague for

thy dowry: be thou as chaste as ice, as pure as

snow, thou shalt not escape calumny. Get thee to a

nunnery, go: farewell. Or, if thou wilt needs

marry, marry a fool; for wise men know well enough

what monsters you make of them. To a nunnery, go,

and quickly too. Farewell.

OPHELIA
O heavenly powers, restore him!

HAMLET
I have heard of your paintings too, well enough; God

has given you one face, and you make yourselves

another: you jig, you amble, and you lisp, and

nick-name God's creatures, and make your wantonness

your ignorance. Go to, I'll no more on't; it hath

made me mad. I say, we will have no more marriages:

those that are married already, all but one, shall

live; the rest shall keep as they are. To a

nunnery, go.

Exit

OPHELIA
O, what a noble mind is here o'erthrown!

The courtier's, soldier's, scholar's, eye, tongue, sword;

The expectancy and rose of the fair state,

The glass of fashion and the mould of form,

The observed of all observers, quite, quite down!

And I, of ladies most deject and wretched,

That suck'd the honey of his music vows,

Now see that noble and most sovereign reason,

Like sweet bells jangled, out of tune and harsh;

That unmatch'd form and feature of blown youth

Blasted with ecstasy: O, woe is me,

To have seen what I have seen, see what I see!

Re-enter KING CLAUDIUS and POLONIUS

KING CLAUDIUS
Love! his affections do not that way tend;

Nor what he spake, though it lack'd form a little,

Was not like madness. There's something in his soul,

O'er which his melancholy sits on brood;

And I do doubt the hatch and the disclose

Will be some danger: which for to prevent,

I have in quick determination

Thus set it down: he shall with speed to England,

For the demand of our neglected tribute

Haply the seas and countries different

With variable objects shall expel

This something-settled matter in his heart,

Whereon his brains still beating puts him thus

From fashion of himself. What think you on't?

LORD POLONIUS
It shall do well: but yet do I believe

The origin and commencement of his grief

Sprung from neglected love. How now, Ophelia!

You need not tell us what Lord Hamlet said;

We heard it all. My lord, do as you please;

But, if you hold it fit, after the play

Let his queen mother all alone entreat him

To show his grief: let her be round with him;

And I'll be placed, so please you, in the ear

Of all their conference. If she find him not,

To England send him, or confine him where

Your wisdom best shall think.

KING CLAUDIUS
It shall be so:

Madness in great ones must not unwatch'd go.

Exeunt

NOTES

NOTES

SCENE II. A hall in the castle.

Enter HAMLET and Players

HAMLET
Speak the speech, I pray you, as I pronounced it to

you, trippingly on the tongue: but if you mouth it,

as many of your players do, I had as lief the

town-crier spoke my lines. Nor do not saw the air

too much with your hand, thus, but use all gently;

for in the very torrent, tempest, and, as I may say,

the whirlwind of passion, you must acquire and beget

a temperance that may give it smoothness. O, it

offends me to the soul to hear a robustious

periwig-pated fellow tear a passion to tatters, to

very rags, to split the ears of the groundlings, who

for the most part are capable of nothing but

inexplicable dumbshows and noise: I would have such

a fellow whipped for o'erdoing Termagant; it

out-herods Herod: pray you, avoid it.

First Player
I warrant your honour.

HAMLET
Be not too tame neither, but let your own discretion

be your tutor: suit the action to the word, the

word to the action; with this special o'erstep not

the modesty of nature: for any thing so overdone is

from the purpose of playing, whose end, both at the

first and now, was and is, to hold, as 'twere, the

mirror up to nature; to show virtue her own feature,

scorn her own image, and the very age and body of

the time his form and pressure. Now this overdone,

or come tardy off, though it make the unskilful

laugh, cannot but make the judicious grieve; the

censure of the which one must in your allowance

o'erweigh a whole theatre of others. O, there be

players that I have seen play, and heard others

praise, and that highly, not to speak it profanely,

that, neither having the accent of Christians nor

the gait of Christian, pagan, nor man, have so

strutted and bellowed that I have thought some of

nature's journeymen had made men and not made them

well, they imitated humanity so abominably.

First Player
I hope we have reformed that indifferently with us,

sir.

HAMLET
O, reform it altogether. And let those that play

your clowns speak no more than is set down for them;

for there be of them that will themselves laugh, to

set on some quantity of barren spectators to laugh

too; though, in the mean time, some necessary

question of the play be then to be considered:

that's villanous, and shows a most pitiful ambition

in the fool that uses it. Go, make you ready.

Exeunt Players
Enter POLONIUS, ROSENCRANTZ, and GUILDENSTERN
How now, my lord! I will the king hear this piece of work?

LORD POLONIUS
And the queen too, and that presently.

HAMLET
Bid the players make haste.

Exit POLONIUS
Will you two help to hasten them?

ROSENCRANTZ GUILDENSTERN
We will, my lord.

Exeunt ROSENCRANTZ and GUILDENSTERN
HAMLET
What ho! Horatio!

Enter HORATIO
HORATIO
Here, sweet lord, at your service.

HAMLET
Horatio, thou art e'en as just a man

As e'er my conversation coped withal.

HORATIO
O, my dear lord,--

HAMLET
Nay, do not think I flatter;

For what advancement may I hope from thee

That no revenue hast but thy good spirits,

To feed and clothe thee? Why should the poor be flatter'd?

No, let the candied tongue lick absurd pomp,

And crook the pregnant hinges of the knee

Where thrift may follow fawning. Dost thou hear?

Since my dear soul was mistress of her choice

And could of men distinguish, her election

Hath seal'd thee for herself; for thou hast been

As one, in suffering all, that suffers nothing,

A man that fortune's buffets and rewards

Hast ta'en with equal thanks: and blest are those

Whose blood and judgment are so well commingled,

That they are not a pipe for fortune's finger

To sound what stop she please. Give me that man

That is not passion's slave, and I will wear him

In my heart's core, ay, in my heart of heart,

As I do thee.--Something too much of this.--

There is a play to-night before the king;

One scene of it comes near the circumstance

Which I have told thee of my father's death:

I prithee, when thou seest that act afoot,

Even with the very comment of thy soul

Observe mine uncle: if his occulted guilt

Do not itself unkennel in one speech,

It is a damned ghost that we have seen,

And my imaginations are as foul

As Vulcan's stithy. Give him heedful note;

For I mine eyes will rivet to his face,

And after we will both our judgments join

In censure of his seeming.

HORATIO
Well, my lord:

If he steal aught the whilst this play is playing,

And 'scape detecting, I will pay the theft.

HAMLET
They are coming to the play; I must be idle:

Get you a place.

Danish march. A flourish. Enter KING CLAUDIUS, QUEEN

GERTRUDE, POLONIUS, OPHELIA, ROSENCRANTZ,

GUILDENSTERN, and others

KING CLAUDIUS
How fares our cousin Hamlet?

HAMLET

Excellent, i' faith; of the chameleon's dish: I eat

the air, promise-crammed: you cannot feed capons so.

KING CLAUDIUS

I have nothing with this answer, Hamlet; these words

are not mine.

HAMLET

No, nor mine now.

To POLONIUS

My lord, you played once i' the university, you say?

LORD POLONIUS

That did I, my lord; and was accounted a good actor.

HAMLET

What did you enact?

LORD POLONIUS

I did enact Julius Caesar: I was killed i' the

Capitol; Brutus killed me.

HAMLET

It was a brute part of him to kill so capital a calf

there. Be the players ready?

ROSENCRANTZ

Ay, my lord; they stay upon your patience.

QUEEN GERTRUDE

Come hither, my dear Hamlet, sit by me.

HAMLET

No, good mother, here's metal more attractive.

LORD POLONIUS

[To KING CLAUDIUS] O, ho! do you mark that?

HAMLET
Lady, shall I lie in your lap?

Lying down at OPHELIA's feet

OPHELIA
No, my lord.

HAMLET
I mean, my head upon your lap?

OPHELIA
Ay, my lord.

HAMLET
Do you think I meant country matters?

OPHELIA
I think nothing, my lord.

HAMLET
That's a fair thought to lie between maids' legs.

OPHELIA
What is, my lord?

HAMLET
Nothing.

OPHELIA
You are merry, my lord.

HAMLET
Who, I?

OPHELIA
Ay, my lord.

HAMLET
O God, your only jig-maker. What should a man do

but be merry? for, look you, how cheerfully my

mother looks, and my father died within these two hours.

OPHELIA
Nay, 'tis twice two months, my lord.

HAMLET
So long? Nay then, let the devil wear black, for

I'll have a suit of sables. O heavens! die two

months ago, and not forgotten yet? Then there's

hope a great man's memory may outlive his life half

a year: but, by'r lady, he must build churches,

then; or else shall he suffer not thinking on, with

the hobby-horse, whose epitaph is 'For, O, for, O,

the hobby-horse is forgot.'

Hautboys play. The dumb-show enters

Enter a King and a Queen very lovingly; the Queen embracing

him, and he her. She kneels, and makes show of protestation

unto him. He takes her up, and declines his head upon her neck:

lays him down upon a bank of flowers: she, seeing him asleep,

leaves him. Anon comes in a fellow, takes off his crown, kisses it,

and pours poison in the King's ears, and exit. The Queen returns;

finds the King dead, and makes passionate action. The Poisoner,

with some two or three Mutes, comes in again, seeming to

lament with her. The dead body is carried away. The Poisoner

wooes the Queen with gifts: she seems loath and unwilling

awhile, but in the end accepts his love

Exeunt

OPHELIA
What means this, my lord?

HAMLET
Marry, this is miching mallecho; it means mischief.

OPHELIA
Belike this show imports the argument of the play.

Enter Prologue

HAMLET
We shall know by this fellow: the players cannot

keep counsel; they'll tell all.

OPHELIA
Will he tell us what this show meant?

HAMLET
Ay, or any show that you'll show him: be not you

ashamed to show, he'll not shame to tell you what it means.

OPHELIA
You are naught, you are naught: I'll mark the play.

Prologue
For us, and for our tragedy,

Here stooping to your clemency,

We beg your hearing patiently.

Exit

HAMLET
Is this a prologue, or the posy of a ring?

OPHELIA
'Tis brief, my lord.

HAMLET
As woman's love.

Enter two Players, King and Queen

Player King
Full thirty times hath Phoebus' cart gone round

Neptune's salt wash and Tellus' orbed ground,

And thirty dozen moons with borrow'd sheen

About the world have times twelve thirties been,

Since love our hearts and Hymen did our hands

Unite commutual in most sacred bands.

Player Queen
So many journeys may the sun and moon

Make us again count o'er ere love be done!

But, woe is me, you are so sick of late,

So far from cheer and from your former state,

That I distrust you. Yet, though I distrust,

Discomfort you, my lord, it nothing must:

For women's fear and love holds quantity;

In neither aught, or in extremity.

Now, what my love is, proof hath made you know;

And as my love is sized, my fear is so:

Where love is great, the littlest doubts are fear;

Where little fears grow great, great love grows there.

Player King
'Faith, I must leave thee, love, and shortly too;

My operant powers their functions leave to do:

And thou shalt live in this fair world behind,

Honour'd, beloved; and haply one as kind

For husband shalt thou--

Player Queen
O, confound the rest!

Such love must needs be treason in my breast:

In second husband let me be accurst!

None wed the second but who kill'd the first.

HAMLET
[Aside] Wormwood, wormwood.

Player Queen
The instances that second marriage move

Are base respects of thrift, but none of love:

A second time I kill my husband dead,

When second husband kisses me in bed.

Player King
I do believe you think what now you speak;

But what we do determine oft we break.

Purpose is but the slave to memory,

Of violent birth, but poor validity;

Which now, like fruit unripe, sticks on the tree;

But fall, unshaken, when they mellow be.

Most necessary 'tis that we forget

To pay ourselves what to ourselves is debt:

What to ourselves in passion we propose,

The passion ending, doth the purpose lose.

The violence of either grief or joy

Their own enactures with themselves destroy:

Where joy most revels, grief doth most lament;

Grief joys, joy grieves, on slender accident.

This world is not for aye, nor 'tis not strange

That even our loves should with our fortunes change;

For 'tis a question left us yet to prove,

Whether love lead fortune, or else fortune love.

The great man down, you mark his favourite flies;

The poor advanced makes friends of enemies.

And hitherto doth love on fortune tend;

For who not needs shall never lack a friend,

And who in want a hollow friend doth try,

Directly seasons him his enemy.

But, orderly to end where I begun,

Our wills and fates do so contrary run

That our devices still are overthrown;

Our thoughts are ours, their ends none of our own:

So think thou wilt no second husband wed;

But die thy thoughts when thy first lord is dead.

Player Queen
Nor earth to me give food, nor heaven light!

Sport and repose lock from me day and night!

To desperation turn my trust and hope!

An anchor's cheer in prison be my scope!

Each opposite that blanks the face of joy

Meet what I would have well and it destroy!

Both here and hence pursue me lasting strife,

If, once a widow, ever I be wife!

HAMLET
If she should break it now!

Player King
'Tis deeply sworn. Sweet, leave me here awhile;

My spirits grow dull, and fain I would beguile

The tedious day with sleep.

Sleeps
Player Queen
Sleep rock thy brain,

And never come mischance between us twain!

Exit
HAMLET
Madam, how like you this play?

QUEEN GERTRUDE
The lady protests too much, methinks.

HAMLET
O, but she'll keep her word.

KING CLAUDIUS
Have you heard the argument? Is there no offence in 't?

HAMLET
No, no, they do but jest, poison in jest; no offence

i' the world.

KING CLAUDIUS
What do you call the play?

HAMLET
The Mouse-trap. Marry, how? Tropically. This play

is the image of a murder done in Vienna: Gonzago is

the duke's name; his wife, Baptista: you shall see

anon; 'tis a knavish piece of work: but what o'

that? your majesty and we that have free souls, it

touches us not: let the galled jade wince, our

withers are unwrung.

Enter LUCIANUS
This is one Lucianus, nephew to the king.

OPHELIA
You are as good as a chorus, my lord.

HAMLET
I could interpret between you and your love, if I

could see the puppets dallying.

OPHELIA
You are keen, my lord, you are keen.

HAMLET
It would cost you a groaning to take off my edge.

OPHELIA
Still better, and worse.

HAMLET
So you must take your husbands. Begin, murderer;

pox, leave thy damnable faces, and begin. Come:

'the croaking raven doth bellow for revenge.'

LUCIANUS
Thoughts black, hands apt, drugs fit, and time agreeing;

Confederate season, else no creature seeing;

Thou mixture rank, of midnight weeds collected,

With Hecate's ban thrice blasted, thrice infected,

Thy natural magic and dire property,

On wholesome life usurp immediately.

Pours the poison into the sleeper's ears

HAMLET
He poisons him i' the garden for's estate. His

name's Gonzago: the story is extant, and writ in

choice Italian: you shall see anon how the murderer

gets the love of Gonzago's wife.

OPHELIA
The king rises.

HAMLET
What, frighted with false fire!

QUEEN GERTRUDE
How fares my lord?

LORD POLONIUS
Give o'er the play.

KING CLAUDIUS
Give me some light: away!

All
Lights, lights, lights!

Exeunt all but HAMLET and HORATIO

HAMLET
Why, let the stricken deer go weep,

The hart ungalled play;

For some must watch, while some must sleep:

So runs the world away.

Would not this, sir, and a forest of feathers-- if

the rest of my fortunes turn Turk with me--with two

Provincial roses on my razed shoes, get me a

fellowship in a cry of players, sir?

HORATIO
Half a share.

HAMLET
A whole one, I.

For thou dost know, O Damon dear,

This realm dismantled was

Of Jove himself; and now reigns here

A very, very--pajock.

HORATIO
You might have rhymed.

HAMLET
O good Horatio, I'll take the ghost's word for a

thousand pound. Didst perceive?

HORATIO
Very well, my lord.

HAMLET
Upon the talk of the poisoning?

HORATIO
I did very well note him.

HAMLET
Ah, ha! Come, some music! come, the recorders!

For if the king like not the comedy,

Why then, belike, he likes it not, perdy.

Come, some music!

Re-enter ROSENCRANTZ and GUILDENSTERN

GUILDENSTERN
Good my lord, vouchsafe me a word with you.

HAMLET
Sir, a whole history.

GUILDENSTERN
The king, sir,--

HAMLET
Ay, sir, what of him?

GUILDENSTERN
Is in his retirement marvellous distempered.

HAMLET
With drink, sir?

GUILDENSTERN
No, my lord, rather with choler.

HAMLET
Your wisdom should show itself more richer to

signify this to his doctor; for, for me to put him

to his purgation would perhaps plunge him into far

more choler.

GUILDENSTERN
Good my lord, put your discourse into some frame and

start not so wildly from my affair.

HAMLET
I am tame, sir: pronounce.

GUILDENSTERN
The queen, your mother, in most great affliction of

spirit, hath sent me to you.

HAMLET
You are welcome.

GUILDENSTERN
Nay, good my lord, this courtesy is not of the right

breed. If it shall please you to make me a

wholesome answer, I will do your mother's

commandment: if not, your pardon and my return

shall be the end of my business.

HAMLET
Sir, I cannot.

GUILDENSTERN
What, my lord?

HAMLET
Make you a wholesome answer; my wit's diseased: but,

sir, such answer as I can make, you shall command;

or, rather, as you say, my mother: therefore no

more, but to the matter: my mother, you say,--

ROSENCRANTZ
Then thus she says; your behavior hath struck her

into amazement and admiration.

HAMLET
O wonderful son, that can so astonish a mother! But

is there no sequel at the heels of this mother's

admiration? Impart.

ROSENCRANTZ
She desires to speak with you in her closet, ere you

go to bed.

HAMLET
We shall obey, were she ten times our mother. Have

you any further trade with us?

ROSENCRANTZ
My lord, you once did love me.

HAMLET
So I do still, by these pickers and stealers.

ROSENCRANTZ
Good my lord, what is your cause of distemper? you

do, surely, bar the door upon your own liberty, if

you deny your griefs to your friend.

HAMLET
Sir, I lack advancement.

ROSENCRANTZ
How can that be, when you have the voice of the king

himself for your succession in Denmark?

HAMLET
Ay, but sir, 'While the grass grows,'--the proverb

is something musty.

Re-enter Players with recorders

O, the recorders! let me see one. To withdraw with

you:--why do you go about to recover the wind of me,

as if you would drive me into a toil?

GUILDENSTERN
O, my lord, if my duty be too bold, my love is too

unmannerly.

HAMLET
I do not well understand that. Will you play upon

this pipe?

GUILDENSTERN
My lord, I cannot.

HAMLET
I pray you.

GUILDENSTERN
Believe me, I cannot.

HAMLET
I do beseech you.

GUILDENSTERN
I know no touch of it, my lord.

HAMLET
'Tis as easy as lying: govern these ventages with

your lingers and thumb, give it breath with your

mouth, and it will discourse most eloquent music.

Look you, these are the stops.

GUILDENSTERN
But these cannot I command to any utterance of

harmony; I have not the skill.

HAMLET
Why, look you now, how unworthy a thing you make of

me! You would play upon me; you would seem to know

my stops; you would pluck out the heart of my

mystery; you would sound me from my lowest note to

the top of my compass: and there is much music,

excellent voice, in this little organ; yet cannot

you make it speak. 'Sblood, do you think I am

easier to be played on than a pipe? Call me what

instrument you will, though you can fret me, yet you

cannot play upon me.

Enter POLONIUS
God bless you, sir!

LORD POLONIUS

My lord, the queen would speak with you, and

presently.

HAMLET

Do you see yonder cloud that's almost in shape of a camel?

LORD POLONIUS

By the mass, and 'tis like a camel, indeed.

HAMLET

Methinks it is like a weasel.

LORD POLONIUS

It is backed like a weasel.

HAMLET

Or like a whale?

LORD POLONIUS

Very like a whale.

HAMLET

Then I will come to my mother by and by. They fool

me to the top of my bent. I will come by and by.

LORD POLONIUS

I will say so.

HAMLET

By and by is easily said.

Exit POLONIUS

Leave me, friends.

Exeunt all but HAMLET

Tis now the very witching time of night,

When churchyards yawn and hell itself breathes out

Contagion to this world: now could I drink hot blood,

And do such bitter business as the day

Would quake to look on. Soft! now to my mother.

O heart, lose not thy nature; let not ever

The soul of Nero enter this firm bosom:

Let me be cruel, not unnatural:

I will speak daggers to her, but use none;

My tongue and soul in this be hypocrites;

How in my words soever she be shent,

To give them seals never, my soul, consent!

Exit

NOTES

SCENE III. A room in the castle.

Enter KING CLAUDIUS, ROSENCRANTZ, and GUILDENSTERN

KING CLAUDIUS

I like him not, nor stands it safe with us

To let his madness range. Therefore prepare you;

I your commission will forthwith dispatch,

And he to England shall along with you:

The terms of our estate may not endure

Hazard so dangerous as doth hourly grow

Out of his lunacies.

GUILDENSTERN

We will ourselves provide:

Most holy and religious fear it is

To keep those many many bodies safe

That live and feed upon your majesty.

ROSENCRANTZ

The single and peculiar life is bound,

With all the strength and armour of the mind,

To keep itself from noyance; but much more

That spirit upon whose weal depend and rest

The lives of many. The cease of majesty

Dies not alone; but, like a gulf, doth draw

What's near it with it: it is a massy wheel,

Fix'd on the summit of the highest mount,

To whose huge spokes ten thousand lesser things

Are mortised and adjoin'd; which, when it falls,

Each small annexment, petty consequence,

Attends the boisterous ruin. Never alone

Did the king sigh, but with a general groan.

KING CLAUDIUS
Arm you, I pray you, to this speedy voyage;

For we will fetters put upon this fear,

Which now goes too free-footed.

ROSENCRANTZ GUILDENSTERN
We will haste us.

Exeunt ROSENCRANTZ and GUILDENSTERN

Enter POLONIUS
LORD POLONIUS
My lord, he's going to his mother's closet:

Behind the arras I'll convey myself,

To hear the process; and warrant she'll tax him home:

And, as you said, and wisely was it said,

'Tis meet that some more audience than a mother,

Since nature makes them partial, should o'erhear

The speech, of vantage. Fare you well, my liege:

I'll call upon you ere you go to bed,

And tell you what I know.

KING CLAUDIUS
Thanks, dear my lord.

Exit POLONIUS

O, my offence is rank it smells to heaven;

It hath the primal eldest curse upon't,

A brother's murder. Pray can I not,

Though inclination be as sharp as will:

My stronger guilt defeats my strong intent;

And, like a man to double business bound,

I stand in pause where I shall first begin,

And both neglect. What if this cursed hand

Were thicker than itself with brother's blood,

Is there not rain enough in the sweet heavens

To wash it white as snow? Whereto serves mercy

But to confront the visage of offence?

And what's in prayer but this two-fold force,

To be forestalled ere we come to fall,

Or pardon'd being down? Then I'll look up;

My fault is past. But, O, what form of prayer

Can serve my turn? 'Forgive me my foul murder'?

That cannot be; since I am still possess'd

Of those effects for which I did the murder,

My crown, mine own ambition and my queen.

May one be pardon'd and retain the offence?

In the corrupted currents of this world

Offence's gilded hand may shove by justice,

And oft 'tis seen the wicked prize itself

Buys out the law: but 'tis not so above;

There is no shuffling, there the action lies

In his true nature; and we ourselves compell'd,

Even to the teeth and forehead of our faults,

To give in evidence. What then? what rests?

Try what repentance can: what can it not?

Yet what can it when one can not repent?

O wretched state! O bosom black as death!

O limed soul, that, struggling to be free,

Art more engaged! Help, angels! Make assay!

Bow, stubborn knees; and, heart with strings of steel,

Be soft as sinews of the newborn babe!

All may be well.

Retires and kneels

Enter HAMLET
HAMLET
Now might I do it pat, now he is praying;

And now I'll do't. And so he goes to heaven;

And so am I revenged. That would be scann'd:

A villain kills my father; and for that,

I, his sole son, do this same villain send

To heaven.

O, this is hire and salary, not revenge.

He took my father grossly, full of bread;

With all his crimes broad blown, as flush as May;

And how his audit stands who knows save heaven?

But in our circumstance and course of thought,

'Tis heavy with him: and am I then revenged,

To take him in the purging of his soul,

When he is fit and season'd for his passage?

No!

Up, sword; and know thou a more horrid hent:

When he is drunk asleep, or in his rage,

Or in the incestuous pleasure of his bed;

At gaming, swearing, or about some act

That has no relish of salvation in't;

Then trip him, that his heels may kick at heaven,

And that his soul may be as damn'd and black

As hell, whereto it goes. My mother stays:

This physic but prolongs thy sickly days.

Exit

KING CLAUDIUS
[Rising] My words fly up, my thoughts remain below:

Words without thoughts never to heaven go.

Exit

<u>*NOTES*</u>

SCENE IV. The Queen's closet.

Enter QUEEN GERTRUDE and POLONIUS

LORD POLONIUS
He will come straight. Look you lay home to him:

Tell him his pranks have been too broad to bear with,

And that your grace hath screen'd and stood between

Much heat and him. I'll sconce me even here.

Pray you, be round with him.

HAMLET
[Within] Mother, mother, mother!

QUEEN GERTRUDE
I'll warrant you,

Fear me not: withdraw, I hear him coming.

POLONIUS hides behind the arras
Enter HAMLET
HAMLET
Now, mother, what's the matter?

QUEEN GERTRUDE
Hamlet, thou hast thy father much offended.

HAMLET
Mother, you have my father much offended.

QUEEN GERTRUDE
Come, come, you answer with an idle tongue.

HAMLET
Go, go, you question with a wicked tongue.

QUEEN GERTRUDE
Why, how now, Hamlet!

HAMLET
What's the matter now?

QUEEN GERTRUDE
Have you forgot me?

HAMLET
No, by the rood, not so:

You are the queen, your husband's brother's wife;

And--would it were not so!--you are my mother.

QUEEN GERTRUDE
Nay, then, I'll set those to you that can speak.

HAMLET
Come, come, and sit you down; you shall not budge;

You go not till I set you up a glass

Where you may see the inmost part of you.

QUEEN GERTRUDE
What wilt thou do? thou wilt not murder me?

Help, help, ho!

LORD POLONIUS
[Behind] What, ho! help, help, help!

HAMLET
[Drawing] How now! a rat? Dead, for a ducat, dead!

Makes a pass through the arras

LORD POLONIUS
[Behind] O, I am slain!

Falls and dies

QUEEN GERTRUDE
O me, what hast thou done?

HAMLET
Nay, I know not:

Is it the king?

QUEEN GERTRUDE
O, what a rash and bloody deed is this!

HAMLET
A bloody deed! almost as bad, good mother,

As kill a king, and marry with his brother.

QUEEN GERTRUDE
As kill a king!

HAMLET
Ay, lady, 'twas my word.

Lifts up the array and discovers POLONIUS

Thou wretched, rash, intruding fool, farewell!

I took thee for thy better: take thy fortune;

Thou find'st to be too busy is some danger.

Leave wringing of your hands: peace! sit you down,

And let me wring your heart; for so I shall,

If it be made of penetrable stuff,

If damned custom have not brass'd it so

That it is proof and bulwark against sense.

QUEEN GERTRUDE
What have I done, that thou darest wag thy tongue

In noise so rude against me?

HAMLET
Such an act

That blurs the grace and blush of modesty,

Calls virtue hypocrite, takes off the rose

From the fair forehead of an innocent love

And sets a blister there, makes marriage-vows

As false as dicers' oaths: O, such a deed

As from the body of contraction plucks

The very soul, and sweet religion makes

A rhapsody of words: heaven's face doth glow:

Yea, this solidity and compound mass,

With tristful visage, as against the doom,

Is thought-sick at the act.

QUEEN GERTRUDE
Ay me, what act,

That roars so loud, and thunders in the index?

HAMLET
Look here, upon this picture, and on this,

The counterfeit presentment of two brothers.

See, what a grace was seated on this brow;

Hyperion's curls; the front of Jove himself;

An eye like Mars, to threaten and command;

A station like the herald Mercury

New-lighted on a heaven-kissing hill;

A combination and a form indeed,

Where every god did seem to set his seal,

To give the world assurance of a man:

This was your husband. Look you now, what follows:

Here is your husband; like a mildew'd ear,

Blasting his wholesome brother. Have you eyes?

Could you on this fair mountain leave to feed,

And batten on this moor? Ha! have you eyes?

You cannot call it love; for at your age

The hey-day in the blood is tame, it's humble,

And waits upon the judgment: and what judgment

Would step from this to this? Sense, sure, you have,

Else could you not have motion; but sure, that sense

Is apoplex'd; for madness would not err,

Nor sense to ecstasy was ne'er so thrall'd

But it reserved some quantity of choice,

To serve in such a difference. What devil was't

That thus hath cozen'd you at hoodman-blind?

Eyes without feeling, feeling without sight,

Ears without hands or eyes, smelling sans all,

Or but a sickly part of one true sense

Could not so mope.

O shame! where is thy blush? Rebellious hell,

If thou canst mutine in a matron's bones,

To flaming youth let virtue be as wax,

And melt in her own fire: proclaim no shame

When the compulsive ardour gives the charge,

Since frost itself as actively doth burn

And reason panders will.

QUEEN GERTRUDE
O Hamlet, speak no more:

Thou turn'st mine eyes into my very soul;

And there I see such black and grained spots

As will not leave their tinct.

HAMLET
Nay, but to live

In the rank sweat of an enseamed bed,

Stew'd in corruption, honeying and making love

Over the nasty sty,--

QUEEN GERTRUDE
O, speak to me no more;

These words, like daggers, enter in mine ears;

No more, sweet Hamlet!

HAMLET
A murderer and a villain;

A slave that is not twentieth part the tithe

Of your precedent lord; a vice of kings;

A cutpurse of the empire and the rule,

That from a shelf the precious diadem stole,

And put it in his pocket!

QUEEN GERTRUDE
No more!

HAMLET
A king of shreds and patches,--

Enter Ghost

Save me, and hover o'er me with your wings,

You heavenly guards! What would your gracious figure?

QUEEN GERTRUDE
Alas, he's mad!

HAMLET
Do you not come your tardy son to chide,

That, lapsed in time and passion, lets go by

The important acting of your dread command? O, say!

Ghost
Do not forget: this visitation

Is but to whet thy almost blunted purpose.

But, look, amazement on thy mother sits:

O, step between her and her fighting soul:

Conceit in weakest bodies strongest works:

Speak to her, Hamlet.

HAMLET
How is it with you, lady?

QUEEN GERTRUDE
Alas, how is't with you,

That you do bend your eye on vacancy

And with the incorporal air do hold discourse?

Forth at your eyes your spirits wildly peep;

And, as the sleeping soldiers in the alarm,

Your bedded hair, like life in excrements,

Starts up, and stands on end. O gentle son,

Upon the heat and flame of thy distemper

Sprinkle cool patience. Whereon do you look?

HAMLET
On him, on him! Look you, how pale he glares!

His form and cause conjoin'd, preaching to stones,

Would make them capable. Do not look upon me;

Lest with this piteous action you convert

My stern effects: then what I have to do

Will want true colour; tears perchance for blood.

QUEEN GERTRUDE
To whom do you speak this?

HAMLET
Do you see nothing there?

QUEEN GERTRUDE
Nothing at all; yet all that is I see.

HAMLET
Nor did you nothing hear?

QUEEN GERTRUDE
No, nothing but ourselves.

HAMLET
Why, look you there! look, how it steals away!

My father, in his habit as he lived!

Look, where he goes, even now, out at the portal!

Exit Ghost

QUEEN GERTRUDE
This the very coinage of your brain:

This bodiless creation ecstasy

Is very cunning in.

HAMLET
Ecstasy!

My pulse, as yours, doth temperately keep time,

And makes as healthful music: it is not madness

That I have utter'd: bring me to the test,

And I the matter will re-word; which madness

Would gambol from. Mother, for love of grace,

Lay not that mattering unction to your soul,

That not your trespass, but my madness speaks:

It will but skin and film the ulcerous place,

Whilst rank corruption, mining all within,

Infects unseen. Confess yourself to heaven;

Repent what's past; avoid what is to come;

And do not spread the compost on the weeds,

To make them ranker. Forgive me this my virtue;

For in the fatness of these pursy times

Virtue itself of vice must pardon beg,

Yea, curb and woo for leave to do him good.

QUEEN GERTRUDE
O Hamlet, thou hast cleft my heart in twain.

HAMLET
O, throw away the worser part of it,

And live the purer with the other half.

Good night: but go not to mine uncle's bed;

Assume a virtue, if you have it not.

That monster, custom, who all sense doth eat,

Of habits devil, is angel yet in this,

That to the use of actions fair and good

He likewise gives a frock or livery,

That aptly is put on. Refrain to-night,

And that shall lend a kind of easiness

To the next abstinence: the next more easy;

For use almost can change the stamp of nature,

And either [ ] the devil, or throw him out

With wondrous potency. Once more, good night:

And when you are desirous to be bless'd,

I'll blessing beg of you. For this same lord,

Pointing to POLONIUS

I do repent: but heaven hath pleased it so,

To punish me with this and this with me,

That I must be their scourge and minister.

I will bestow him, and will answer well

The death I gave him. So, again, good night.

I must be cruel, only to be kind:

Thus bad begins and worse remains behind.

One word more, good lady.

QUEEN GERTRUDE
What shall I do?

HAMLET
Not this, by no means, that I bid you do:

Let the bloat king tempt you again to bed;

Pinch wanton on your cheek; call you his mouse;

And let him, for a pair of reechy kisses,

Or paddling in your neck with his damn'd fingers,

Make you to ravel all this matter out,

That I essentially am not in madness,

But mad in craft. 'Twere good you let him know;

For who, that's but a queen, fair, sober, wise,

Would from a paddock, from a bat, a gib,

Such dear concernings hide? who would do so?

No, in despite of sense and secrecy,

Unpeg the basket on the house's top.

Let the birds fly, and, like the famous ape,

To try conclusions, in the basket creep,

And break your own neck down.

QUEEN GERTRUDE
Be thou assured, if words be made of breath,

And breath of life, I have no life to breathe

What thou hast said to me.

HAMLET
I must to England; you know that?

QUEEN GERTRUDE
Alack,

I had forgot: 'tis so concluded on.

HAMLET
There's letters seal'd: and my two schoolfellows,

Whom I will trust as I will adders fang'd,

They bear the mandate; they must sweep my way,

And marshal me to knavery. Let it work;

For 'tis the sport to have the engineer

Hoist with his own petard: and 't shall go hard

But I will delve one yard below their mines,

And blow them at the moon: O, 'tis most sweet,

When in one line two crafts directly meet.

This man shall set me packing:

I'll lug the guts into the neighbour room.

Mother, good night. Indeed this counsellor

Is now most still, most secret and most grave,

Who was in life a foolish prating knave.

Come, sir, to draw toward an end with you.

Good night, mother.

Exeunt severally; HAMLET dragging in POLONIUS

NOTES

NOTES

NOTES

ACT IV

SCENE I. A room in the castle.

Enter KING CLAUDIUS, QUEEN GERTRUDE, ROSENCRANTZ, and

GUILDENSTERN

KING CLAUDIUS
There's matter in these sighs, these profound heaves:

You must translate: 'tis fit we understand them.

Where is your son?

QUEEN GERTRUDE
Bestow this place on us a little while.

Exeunt ROSENCRANTZ and GUILDENSTERN
Ah, my good lord, what have I seen to-night!

KING CLAUDIUS
What, Gertrude? How does Hamlet?

QUEEN GERTRUDE
Mad as the sea and wind, when both contend

Which is the mightier: in his lawless fit,

Behind the arras hearing something stir,

Whips out his rapier, cries, 'A rat, a rat!'

And, in this brainish apprehension, kills

The unseen good old man.

KING CLAUDIUS
O heavy deed!

It had been so with us, had we been there:

His liberty is full of threats to all;

To you yourself, to us, to every one.

Alas, how shall this bloody deed be answer'd?

It will be laid to us, whose providence

Should have kept short, restrain'd and out of haunt,

This mad young man: but so much was our love,

We would not understand what was most fit;

But, like the owner of a foul disease,

To keep it from divulging, let it feed

Even on the pith of Life. Where is he gone?

QUEEN GERTRUDE
To draw apart the body he hath kill'd:

O'er whom his very madness, like some ore

Among a mineral of metals base,

Shows itself pure; he weeps for what is done.

KING CLAUDIUS
O Gertrude, come away!

The sun no sooner shall the mountains touch,

But we will ship him hence: and this vile deed

We must, with all our majesty and skill,

Both countenance and excuse. Ho, Guildenstern!

Re-enter ROSENCRANTZ and GUILDENSTERN
Friends both, go join you with some further aid:

Hamlet in madness hath Polonius slain,

And from his mother's closet hath he dragg'd him:

Go seek him out; speak fair, and bring the body

Into the chapel. I pray you, haste in this.

Exeunt ROSENCRANTZ and GUILDENSTERN

Come, Gertrude, we'll call up our wisest friends;

And let them know, both what we mean to do,

And what's untimely done. O, come away!

My soul is full of discord and dismay.

Exeunt

<u>*NOTES*</u>

SCENE II. Another room in the castle.

Enter HAMLET

HAMLET
Safely stowed.

ROSENCRANTZ: GUILDENSTERN:
[Within] Hamlet! Lord Hamlet!

HAMLET
What noise? who calls on Hamlet?

O, here they come.

Enter ROSENCRANTZ and GUILDENSTERN

ROSENCRANTZ
What have you done, my lord, with the dead body?

HAMLET
Compounded it with dust, whereto 'tis kin.

ROSENCRANTZ
Tell us where 'tis, that we may take it thence

And bear it to the chapel.

HAMLET
Do not believe it.

ROSENCRANTZ
Believe what?

HAMLET
That I can keep your counsel and not mine own.

Besides, to be demanded of a sponge! what

replication should be made by the son of a king?

ROSENCRANTZ
Take you me for a sponge, my lord?

HAMLET
Ay, sir, that soaks up the king's countenance, his

rewards, his authorities. But such officers do the

king best service in the end: he keeps them, like

an ape, in the corner of his jaw; first mouthed, to

be last swallowed: when he needs what you have

gleaned, it is but squeezing you, and, sponge, you

shall be dry again.

ROSENCRANTZ
I understand you not, my lord.

HAMLET
I am glad of it: a knavish speech sleeps in a

foolish ear.

ROSENCRANTZ
My lord, you must tell us where the body is, and go

with us to the king.

HAMLET
The body is with the king, but the king is not with

the body. The king is a thing--

GUILDENSTERN
A thing, my lord!

HAMLET
Of nothing: bring me to him. Hide fox, and all after.

Exeunt

NOTES

SCENE III. Another room in the castle.

Enter KING CLAUDIUS, attended

KING CLAUDIUS
I have sent to seek him, and to find the body.

How dangerous is it that this man goes loose!

Yet must not we put the strong law on him:

He's loved of the distracted multitude,

Who like not in their judgment, but their eyes;

And where tis so, the offender's scourge is weigh'd,

But never the offence. To bear all smooth and even,

This sudden sending him away must seem

Deliberate pause: diseases desperate grown

By desperate appliance are relieved,

Or not at all.

Enter ROSENCRANTZ

How now! what hath befall'n?

ROSENCRANTZ
Where the dead body is bestow'd, my lord,

We cannot get from him.

KING CLAUDIUS
But where is he?

ROSENCRANTZ
Without, my lord; guarded, to know your pleasure.

KING CLAUDIUS
Bring him before us.

ROSENCRANTZ
Ho, Guildenstern! bring in my lord.

Enter HAMLET and GUILDENSTERN

KING CLAUDIUS
Now, Hamlet, where's Polonius?

HAMLET
At supper.

KING CLAUDIUS
At supper! where?

HAMLET
Not where he eats, but where he is eaten: a certain

convocation of politic worms are e'en at him. Your

worm is your only emperor for diet: we fat all

creatures else to fat us, and we fat ourselves for

maggots: your fat king and your lean beggar is but

variable service, two dishes, but to one table:

that's the end.

KING CLAUDIUS
Alas, alas!

HAMLET
A man may fish with the worm that hath eat of a

king, and eat of the fish that hath fed of that worm.

KING CLAUDIUS
What dost you mean by this?

HAMLET
Nothing but to show you how a king may go a

progress through the guts of a beggar.

KING CLAUDIUS
Where is Polonius?

HAMLET
In heaven; send hither to see: if your messenger

find him not there, seek him i' the other place

yourself. But indeed, if you find him not within

this month, you shall nose him as you go up the

stairs into the lobby.

KING CLAUDIUS
Go seek him there.

To some Attendants

HAMLET
He will stay till ye come.

Exeunt Attendants

KING CLAUDIUS
Hamlet, this deed, for thine especial safety,--

Which we do tender, as we dearly grieve

For that which thou hast done,--must send thee hence

With fiery quickness: therefore prepare thyself;

The bark is ready, and the wind at help,

The associates tend, and every thing is bent

For England.

HAMLET
For England!

KING CLAUDIUS
Ay, Hamlet.

HAMLET
Good.

KING CLAUDIUS
So is it, if thou knew'st our purposes.

HAMLET
I see a cherub that sees them. But, come; for

England! Farewell, dear mother.

KING CLAUDIUS
Thy loving father, Hamlet.

HAMLET
My mother: father and mother is man and wife; man

and wife is one flesh; and so, my mother. Come, for England!

Exit

KING CLAUDIUS
Follow him at foot; tempt him with speed aboard;

Delay it not; I'll have him hence to-night:

Away! for every thing is seal'd and done

That else leans on the affair: pray you, make haste.

Exeunt ROSENCRANTZ and GUILDENSTERN

And, England, if my love thou hold'st at aught--

As my great power thereof may give thee sense,

Since yet thy cicatrice looks raw and red

After the Danish sword, and thy free awe

Pays homage to us--thou mayst not coldly set

Our sovereign process; which imports at full,

By letters congruing to that effect,

The present death of Hamlet. Do it, England;

For like the hectic in my blood he rages,

And thou must cure me: till I know 'tis done,

Howe'er my haps, my joys were ne'er begun.

Exit

<u>*NOTES*</u>

SCENE IV. A plain in Denmark.

Enter FORTINBRAS, a Captain, and Soldiers, marching

PRINCE FORTINBRAS
Go, captain, from me greet the Danish king;

Tell him that, by his licence, Fortinbras

Craves the conveyance of a promised march

Over his kingdom. You know the rendezvous.

If that his majesty would aught with us,

We shall express our duty in his eye;

And let him know so.

Captain
I will do't, my lord.

PRINCE FORTINBRAS
Go softly on.

Exeunt FORTINBRAS and Soldiers

Enter HAMLET, ROSENCRANTZ, GUILDENSTERN, and others

HAMLET
Good sir, whose powers are these?

Captain
They are of Norway, sir.

HAMLET
How purposed, sir, I pray you?

Captain
Against some part of Poland.

HAMLET
Who commands them, sir?

Captain
The nephews to old Norway, Fortinbras.

HAMLET
Goes it against the main of Poland, sir,

Or for some frontier?

Captain
Truly to speak, and with no addition,

We go to gain a little patch of ground

That hath in it no profit but the name.

To pay five ducats, five, I would not farm it;

Nor will it yield to Norway or the Pole

A ranker rate, should it be sold in fee.

HAMLET
Why, then the Polack never will defend it.

Captain
Yes, it is already garrison'd.

HAMLET
Two thousand souls and twenty thousand ducats

Will not debate the question of this straw:

This is the imposthume of much wealth and peace,

That inward breaks, and shows no cause without

Why the man dies. I humbly thank you, sir.

Captain
God be wi' you, sir.

Exit

ROSENCRANTZ
Wilt please you go, my lord?

HAMLET
I'll be with you straight go a little before.

Exeunt all except HAMLET

How all occasions do inform against me,

And spur my dull revenge! What is a man,

If his chief good and market of his time

Be but to sleep and feed? a beast, no more.

Sure, he that made us with such large discourse,

Looking before and after, gave us not

That capability and god-like reason

To fust in us unused. Now, whether it be

Bestial oblivion, or some craven scruple

Of thinking too precisely on the event,

A thought which, quarter'd, hath but one part wisdom

And ever three parts coward, I do not know

Why yet I live to say 'This thing's to do;'

Sith I have cause and will and strength and means

To do't. Examples gross as earth exhort me:

Witness this army of such mass and charge

Led by a delicate and tender prince,

Whose spirit with divine ambition puff'd

Makes mouths at the invisible event,

Exposing what is mortal and unsure

To all that fortune, death and danger dare,

Even for an egg-shell. Rightly to be great

Is not to stir without great argument,

But greatly to find quarrel in a straw

When honour's at the stake. How stand I then,

That have a father kill'd, a mother stain'd,

Excitements of my reason and my blood,

And let all sleep? while, to my shame, I see

The imminent death of twenty thousand men,

That, for a fantasy and trick of fame,

Go to their graves like beds, fight for a plot

Whereon the numbers cannot try the cause,

Which is not tomb enough and continent

To hide the slain? O, from this time forth,

My thoughts be bloody, or be nothing worth!

Exit

NOTES

NOTES

SCENE V. Elsinore. A room in the castle.

Enter QUEEN GERTRUDE, HORATIO, and a Gentleman

QUEEN GERTRUDE
I will not speak with her.

Gentleman
She is importunate, indeed distract:

Her mood will needs be pitied.

QUEEN GERTRUDE
What would she have?

Gentleman
She speaks much of her father; says she hears

There's tricks i' the world; and hems, and beats her heart;

Spurns enviously at straws; speaks things in doubt,

That carry but half sense: her speech is nothing,

Yet the unshaped use of it doth move

The hearers to collection; they aim at it,

And botch the words up fit to their own thoughts;

Which, as her winks, and nods, and gestures

yield them,

Indeed would make one think there might be thought,

Though nothing sure, yet much unhappily.

HORATIO
'Twere good she were spoken with; for she may strew

Dangerous conjectures in ill-breeding minds.

QUEEN GERTRUDE
Let her come in.

Exit HORATIO

To my sick soul, as sin's true nature is,

Each toy seems prologue to some great amiss:

So full of artless jealousy is guilt,

It spills itself in fearing to be spilt.

Re-enter HORATIO, with OPHELIA

OPHELIA
Where is the beauteous majesty of Denmark?

QUEEN GERTRUDE
How now, Ophelia!

OPHELIA
[Sings]

How should I your true love know

From another one?

By his cockle hat and staff,

And his sandal shoon.

QUEEN GERTRUDE
Alas, sweet lady, what imports this song?

OPHELIA
Say you? nay, pray you, mark.

Sings

He is dead and gone, lady,

He is dead and gone;

At his head a grass-green turf,

At his heels a stone.

QUEEN GERTRUDE
Nay, but, Ophelia,--

OPHELIA
Pray you, mark.

Sings

White his shroud as the mountain snow,--

Enter KING CLAUDIUS
QUEEN GERTRUDE
Alas, look here, my lord.

OPHELIA
[Sings]

Larded with sweet flowers

Which bewept to the grave did go

With true-love showers.

KING CLAUDIUS
How do you, pretty lady?

OPHELIA
Well, God 'ild you! They say the owl was a baker's

daughter. Lord, we know what we are, but know not

what we may be. God be at your table!

KING CLAUDIUS
Conceit upon her father.

OPHELIA
Pray you, let's have no words of this; but when they

ask you what it means, say you this:

Sings

To-morrow is Saint Valentine's day,

All in the morning betime,

And I a maid at your window,

To be your Valentine.

Then up he rose, and donn'd his clothes,

And dupp'd the chamber-door;

Let in the maid, that out a maid

Never departed more.

KING CLAUDIUS
Pretty Ophelia!

OPHELIA
Indeed, la, without an oath, I'll make an end on't:

Sings
By Gis and by Saint Charity,

Alack, and fie for shame!

Young men will do't, if they come to't;

By cock, they are to blame.

Quoth she, before you tumbled me,

You promised me to wed.

So would I ha' done, by yonder sun,

An thou hadst not come to my bed.

KING CLAUDIUS
How long hath she been thus?

OPHELIA

I hope all will be well. We must be patient: but I

cannot choose but weep, to think they should lay him

i' the cold ground. My brother shall know of it:

and so I thank you for your good counsel. Come, my

coach! Good night, ladies; good night, sweet ladies;

good night, good night.

Exit

KING CLAUDIUS

Follow her close; give her good watch,

I pray you.

Exit HORATIO

O, this is the poison of deep grief; it springs

All from her father's death. O Gertrude, Gertrude,

When sorrows come, they come not single spies

But in battalions. First, her father slain:

Next, your son gone; and he most violent author

Of his own just remove: the people muddied,

Thick and unwholesome in their thoughts and whispers,

For good Polonius' death; and we have done but greenly,

In hugger-mugger to inter him: poor Ophelia

Divided from herself and her fair judgment,

Without the which we are pictures, or mere beasts:

Last, and as much containing as all these,

Her brother is in secret come from France;

Feeds on his wonder, keeps himself in clouds,

And wants not buzzers to infect his ear

With pestilent speeches of his father's death;

Wherein necessity, of matter beggar'd,

Will nothing stick our person to arraign

In ear and ear. O my dear Gertrude, this,

Like to a murdering-piece, in many places

Gives me superfluous death.

A noise within
QUEEN GERTRUDE
Alack, what noise is this?

KING CLAUDIUS
Where are my Switzers? Let them guard the door.

Enter another Gentleman

What is the matter?

Gentleman
Save yourself, my lord:

The ocean, overpeering of his list,

Eats not the flats with more impetuous haste

Than young Laertes, in a riotous head,

O'erbears your officers. The rabble call him lord;

And, as the world were now but to begin,

Antiquity forgot, custom not known,

The ratifiers and props of every word,

They cry 'Choose we: Laertes shall be king:'

Caps, hands, and tongues, applaud it to the clouds:

'Laertes shall be king, Laertes king!'

QUEEN GERTRUDE
How cheerfully on the false trail they cry!

O, this is counter, you false Danish dogs!

KING CLAUDIUS
The doors are broke.

Noise within

Enter LAERTES, armed; Danes following
LAERTES
Where is this king? Sirs, stand you all without.

Danes
No, let's come in.

LAERTES
I pray you, give me leave.

Danes
We will, we will.

They retire without the door

LAERTES
I thank you: keep the door. O thou vile king,

Give me my father!

QUEEN GERTRUDE
Calmly, good Laertes.

LAERTES
That drop of blood that's calm proclaims me bastard,

Cries cuckold to my father, brands the harlot

Even here, between the chaste unsmirched brow

Of my true mother.

KING CLAUDIUS
What is the cause, Laertes,

That thy rebellion looks so giant-like?

Let him go, Gertrude; do not fear our person:

There's such divinity doth hedge a king,

That treason can but peep to what it would,

Acts little of his will. Tell me, Laertes,

Why thou art thus incensed. Let him go, Gertrude.

Speak, man.

LAERTES
Where is my father?

KING CLAUDIUS
Dead.

QUEEN GERTRUDE
But not by him.

KING CLAUDIUS
Let him demand his fill.

LAERTES
How came he dead? I'll not be juggled with:

To hell, allegiance! vows, to the blackest devil!

Conscience and grace, to the profoundest pit!

I dare damnation. To this point I stand,

That both the worlds I give to negligence,

Let come what comes; only I'll be revenged

Most thoroughly for my father.

KING CLAUDIUS
Who shall stay you?

LAERTES
My will, not all the world:

And for my means, I'll husband them so well,

They shall go far with little.

KING CLAUDIUS
Good Laertes,

If you desire to know the certainty

Of your dear father's death, is't writ in your revenge,

That, swoopstake, you will draw both friend and foe,

Winner and loser?

LAERTES
None but his enemies.

KING CLAUDIUS
Will you know them then?

LAERTES
To his good friends thus wide I'll ope my arms;

And like the kind life-rendering pelican,

Repast them with my blood.

KING CLAUDIUS
Why, now you speak

Like a good child and a true gentleman.

That I am guiltless of your father's death,

And am most sensible in grief for it,

It shall as level to your judgment pierce

As day does to your eye.

Danes
[Within] Let her come in.

LAERTES
How now! what noise is that?

Re-enter OPHELIA

O heat, dry up my brains! tears seven times salt,

Burn out the sense and virtue of mine eye!

By heaven, thy madness shall be paid by weight,

Till our scale turn the beam. O rose of May!

Dear maid, kind sister, sweet Ophelia!

O heavens! is't possible, a young maid's wits

Should be as moral as an old man's life?

Nature is fine in love, and where 'tis fine,

It sends some precious instance of itself

After the thing it loves.

OPHELIA
[Sings]

They bore him barefaced on the bier;

Hey non nonny, nonny, hey nonny;

And in his grave rain'd many a tear:--

Fare you well, my dove!

LAERTES
Hadst thou thy wits, and didst persuade revenge,

It could not move thus.

OPHELIA
[Sings]

You must sing a-down a-down,

An you call him a-down-a.

O, how the wheel becomes it! It is the false

steward, that stole his master's daughter.

LAERTES
This nothing's more than matter.

OPHELIA
There's rosemary, that's for remembrance; pray,

love, remember: and there is pansies. that's for thoughts.

LAERTES
A document in madness, thoughts and remembrance fitted.

OPHELIA
There's fennel for you, and columbines: there's rue

for you; and here's some for me: we may call it

herb-grace o' Sundays: O you must wear your rue with

a difference. There's a daisy: I would give you

some violets, but they withered all when my father

died: they say he made a good end,--

Sings

For bonny sweet Robin is all my joy.

LAERTES
Thought and affliction, passion, hell itself,

She turns to favour and to prettiness.

OPHELIA
[Sings]

And will he not come again?

And will he not come again?

No, no, he is dead:

Go to thy death-bed:

He never will come again.

His beard was as white as snow,

All flaxen was his poll:

He is gone, he is gone,

And we cast away moan:

God ha' mercy on his soul!

And of all Christian souls, I pray God. God be wi' ye.

Exit

LAERTES
Do you see this, O God?

KING CLAUDIUS
Laertes, I must commune with your grief,

Or you deny me right. Go but apart,

Make choice of whom your wisest friends you will.

And they shall hear and judge 'twixt you and me:

If by direct or by collateral hand

They find us touch'd, we will our kingdom give,

Our crown, our life, and all that we can ours,

To you in satisfaction; but if not,

Be you content to lend your patience to us,

And we shall jointly labour with your soul

To give it due content.

LAERTES
Let this be so;

His means of death, his obscure funeral--

No trophy, sword, nor hatchment o'er his bones,

No noble rite nor formal ostentation--

Cry to be heard, as 'twere from heaven to earth,

That I must call't in question.

KING CLAUDIUS
So you shall;

And where the offence is let the great axe fall.

I pray you, go with me.

Exeunt

SCENE VI. Another room in the castle.

Enter HORATIO and a Servant

HORATIO
What are they that would speak with me?

Servant
Sailors, sir: they say they have letters for you.

HORATIO
Let them come in.

Exit Servant

I do not know from what part of the world

I should be greeted, if not from Lord Hamlet.

Enter Sailors
First Sailor
God bless you, sir.

HORATIO
Let him bless thee too.

First Sailor
He shall, sir, an't please him. There's a letter for

you, sir; it comes from the ambassador that was

bound for England; if your name be Horatio, as I am

let to know it is.

HORATIO
[Reads] 'Horatio, when thou shalt have overlooked

this, give these fellows some means to the king:

they have letters for him. Ere we were two days old

at sea, a pirate of very warlike appointment gave us

chase. Finding ourselves too slow of sail, we put on

a compelled valour, and in the grapple I boarded

them: on the instant they got clear of our ship; so

I alone became their prisoner. They have dealt with

me like thieves of mercy: but they knew what they

did; I am to do a good turn for them. Let the king

have the letters I have sent; and repair thou to me

with as much speed as thou wouldst fly death. I

have words to speak in thine ear will make thee

dumb; yet are they much too light for the bore of

the matter. These good fellows will bring thee

where I am. Rosencrantz and Guildenstern hold their

course for England: of them I have much to tell

thee. Farewell.

'He that thou knowest thine, HAMLET.'

Come, I will make you way for these your letters;

And do't the speedier, that you may direct me

To him from whom you brought them.

Exeunt

NOTES

SCENE VII. Another room in the castle.

Enter KING CLAUDIUS and LAERTES

KING CLAUDIUS
Now must your conscience my acquaintance seal,

And you must put me in your heart for friend,

Sith you have heard, and with a knowing ear,

That he which hath your noble father slain

Pursued my life.

LAERTES
It well appears: but tell me

Why you proceeded not against these feats,

So crimeful and so capital in nature,

As by your safety, wisdom, all things else,

You mainly were stirr'd up.

KING CLAUDIUS
O, for two special reasons;

Which may to you, perhaps, seem much unsinew'd,

But yet to me they are strong. The queen his mother

Lives almost by his looks; and for myself--

My virtue or my plague, be it either which--

She's so conjunctive to my life and soul,

That, as the star moves not but in his sphere,

I could not but by her. The other motive,

Why to a public count I might not go,

Is the great love the general gender bear him;

Who, dipping all his faults in their affection,

Would, like the spring that turneth wood to stone,

Convert his gyves to graces; so that my arrows,

Too slightly timber'd for so loud a wind,

Would have reverted to my bow again,

And not where I had aim'd them.

LAERTES
And so have I a noble father lost;

A sister driven into desperate terms,

Whose worth, if praises may go back again,

Stood challenger on mount of all the age

For her perfections: but my revenge will come.

KING CLAUDIUS
Break not your sleeps for that: you must not think

That we are made of stuff so flat and dull

That we can let our beard be shook with danger

And think it pastime. You shortly shall hear more:

I loved your father, and we love ourself;

And that, I hope, will teach you to imagine--

Enter a Messenger
How now! what news?

Messenger
Letters, my lord, from Hamlet:

This to your majesty; this to the queen.

KING CLAUDIUS
From Hamlet! who brought them?

Messenger
Sailors, my lord, they say; I saw them not:

They were given me by Claudio; he received them

Of him that brought them.

KING CLAUDIUS
Laertes, you shall hear them. Leave us.

Exit Messenger

Reads

'High and mighty, You shall know I am set naked on

your kingdom. To-morrow shall I beg leave to see

your kingly eyes: when I shall, first asking your

pardon thereunto, recount the occasion of my sudden

and more strange return. 'HAMLET.'

What should this mean? Are all the rest come back?

Or is it some abuse, and no such thing?

LAERTES
Know you the hand?

KING CLAUDIUS
'Tis Hamlets character. 'Naked!

And in a postscript here, he says 'alone.'

Can you advise me?

LAERTES
I'm lost in it, my lord. But let him come;

It warms the very sickness in my heart,

That I shall live and tell him to his teeth,

'Thus didest thou.'

KING CLAUDIUS
If it be so, Laertes--

As how should it be so? how otherwise?--

Will you be ruled by me?

LAERTES
Ay, my lord;

So you will not o'errule me to a peace.

KING CLAUDIUS
To thine own peace. If he be now return'd,

As checking at his voyage, and that he means

No more to undertake it, I will work him

To an exploit, now ripe in my device,

Under the which he shall not choose but fall:

And for his death no wind of blame shall breathe,

But even his mother shall uncharge the practise

And call it accident.

LAERTES
My lord, I will be ruled;

The rather, if you could devise it so

That I might be the organ.

KING CLAUDIUS
It falls right.

You have been talk'd of since your travel much,

And that in Hamlet's hearing, for a quality

Wherein, they say, you shine: your sum of parts

Did not together pluck such envy from him

As did that one, and that, in my regard,

Of the unworthiest siege.

LAERTES
What part is that, my lord?

KING CLAUDIUS
A very riband in the cap of youth,

Yet needful too; for youth no less becomes

The light and careless livery that it wears

Than settled age his sables and his weeds,

Importing health and graveness. Two months since,

Here was a gentleman of Normandy:--

I've seen myself, and served against, the French,

And they can well on horseback: but this gallant

Had witchcraft in't; he grew unto his seat;

And to such wondrous doing brought his horse,

As he had been incorpsed and demi-natured

With the brave beast: so far he topp'd my thought,

That I, in forgery of shapes and tricks,

Come short of what he did.

LAERTES
A Norman was't?

KING CLAUDIUS
A Norman.

LAERTES
Upon my life, Lamond.

KING CLAUDIUS
The very same.

LAERTES
I know him well: he is the brooch indeed

And gem of all the nation.

KING CLAUDIUS
He made confession of you,

And gave you such a masterly report

For art and exercise in your defence

And for your rapier most especially,

That he cried out, 'twould be a sight indeed,

If one could match you: the scrimers of their nation,

He swore, had had neither motion, guard, nor eye,

If you opposed them. Sir, this report of his

Did Hamlet so envenom with his envy

That he could nothing do but wish and beg

Your sudden coming o'er, to play with him.

Now, out of this,--

LAERTES
What out of this, my lord?

KING CLAUDIUS
Laertes, was your father dear to you?

Or are you like the painting of a sorrow,

A face without a heart?

LAERTES
Why ask you this?

KING CLAUDIUS
Not that I think you did not love your father;

But that I know love is begun by time;

And that I see, in passages of proof,

Time qualifies the spark and fire of it.

There lives within the very flame of love

A kind of wick or snuff that will abate it;

And nothing is at a like goodness still;

For goodness, growing to a plurisy,

Dies in his own too much: that we would do

We should do when we would; for this 'would' changes

And hath abatements and delays as many

As there are tongues, are hands, are accidents;

And then this 'should' is like a spendthrift sigh,

That hurts by easing. But, to the quick o' the ulcer:--

Hamlet comes back: what would you undertake,

To show yourself your father's son in deed

More than in words?

LAERTES
To cut his throat i' the church.

KING CLAUDIUS
No place, indeed, should murder sanctuarize;

Revenge should have no bounds. But, good Laertes,

Will you do this, keep close within your chamber.

Hamlet return'd shall know you are come home:

We'll put on those shall praise your excellence

And set a double varnish on the fame

The Frenchman gave you, bring you in fine together

And wager on your heads: he, being remiss,

Most generous and free from all contriving,

Will not peruse the foils; so that, with ease,

Or with a little shuffling, you may choose

A sword unbated, and in a pass of practise

Requite him for your father.

LAERTES
I will do't:

And, for that purpose, I'll anoint my sword.

I bought an unction of a mountebank,

So mortal that, but dip a knife in it,

Where it draws blood no cataplasm so rare,

Collected from all simples that have virtue

Under the moon, can save the thing from death

That is but scratch'd withal: I'll touch my point

With this contagion, that, if I gall him slightly,

It may be death.

KING CLAUDIUS
Let's further think of this;

Weigh what convenience both of time and means

May fit us to our shape: if this should fail,

And that our drift look through our bad performance,

'Twere better not assay'd: therefore this project

Should have a back or second, that might hold,

If this should blast in proof. Soft! let me see:

We'll make a solemn wager on your cunnings: I ha't.

When in your motion you are hot and dry--

As make your bouts more violent to that end--

And that he calls for drink, I'll have prepared him

A chalice for the nonce, whereon but sipping,

If he by chance escape your venom'd stuck,

Our purpose may hold there.

Enter QUEEN GERTRUDE
How now, sweet queen!

QUEEN GERTRUDE
One woe doth tread upon another's heel,

So fast they follow; your sister's drown'd, Laertes.

LAERTES
Drown'd! O, where?

QUEEN GERTRUDE
There is a willow grows aslant a brook,

That shows his hoar leaves in the glassy stream;

There with fantastic garlands did she come

Of crow-flowers, nettles, daisies, and long purples

That liberal shepherds give a grosser name,

But our cold maids do dead men's fingers call them:

There, on the pendent boughs her coronet weeds

Clambering to hang, an envious sliver broke;

When down her weedy trophies and herself

Fell in the weeping brook. Her clothes spread wide;

And, mermaid-like, awhile they bore her up:

Which time she chanted snatches of old tunes;

As one incapable of her own distress,

Or like a creature native and indued

Unto that element: but long it could not be

Till that her garments, heavy with their drink,

Pull'd the poor wretch from her melodious lay

To muddy death.

LAERTES
Alas, then, she is drown'd?

QUEEN GERTRUDE
Drown'd, drown'd.

LAERTES
Too much of water hast thou, poor Ophelia,

And therefore I forbid my tears: but yet

It is our trick; nature her custom holds,

Let shame say what it will: when these are gone,

The woman will be out. Adieu, my lord:

I have a speech of fire, that fain would blaze,

But that this folly douts it.

Exit

KING CLAUDIUS
Let's follow, Gertrude:

How much I had to do to calm his rage!

Now fear I this will give it start again;

Therefore let's follow.

Exeunt

NOTES

NOTES

NOTES

ACT V

SCENE I. A churchyard.

Enter two Clowns, with spades, & c

First Clown
Is she to be buried in Christian burial that

wilfully seeks her own salvation?

Second Clown
I tell thee she is: and therefore make her grave

straight: the crowner hath sat on her, and finds it

Christian burial.

First Clown
How can that be, unless she drowned herself in her

own defence?

Second Clown
Why, 'tis found so.

First Clown
It must be 'se offendendo;' it cannot be else. For

here lies the point: if I drown myself wittingly,

it argues an act: and an act hath three branches: it

is, to act, to do, to perform: argal, she drowned

herself wittingly.

Second Clown
Nay, but hear you, goodman delver,--

First Clown
Give me leave. Here lies the water; good: here

stands the man; good; if the man go to this water,

and drown himself, it is, will he, nill he, he

goes,--mark you that; but if the water come to him

and drown him, he drowns not himself: argal, he

that is not guilty of his own death shortens not his own life.

Second Clown
But is this law?

First Clown
Ay, marry, is't; crowner's quest law.

Second Clown
Will you ha' the truth on't? If this had not been

a gentlewoman, she should have been buried out o'

Christian burial.

First Clown
Why, there thou say'st: and the more pity that

great folk should have countenance in this world to

drown or hang themselves, more than their even

Christian. Come, my spade. There is no ancient

gentleman but gardeners, ditchers, and grave-makers:

they hold up Adam's profession.

Second Clown
Was he a gentleman?

First Clown
He was the first that ever bore arms.

Second Clown
Why, he had none.

First Clown
What, art a heathen? How dost thou understand the

Scripture? The Scripture says 'Adam digged:'

could he dig without arms? I'll put another

question to thee: if thou answerest me not to the

purpose, confess thyself--

Second Clown
Go to.

First Clown
What is he that builds stronger than either the

mason, the shipwright, or the carpenter?

Second Clown
The gallows-maker; for that frame outlives a

thousand tenants.

First Clown
I like thy wit well, in good faith: the gallows

does well; but how does it well? it does well to

those that do in: now thou dost ill to say the

gallows is built stronger than the church: argal,

the gallows may do well to thee. To't again, come.

Second Clown
'Who builds stronger than a mason, a shipwright, or

a carpenter?'

First Clown
Ay, tell me that, and unyoke.

Second Clown
Marry, now I can tell.

First Clown
To't.

Second Clown
Mass, I cannot tell.

Enter HAMLET and HORATIO, at a distance

First Clown
Cudgel thy brains no more about it, for your dull

ass will not mend his pace with beating; and, when

you are asked this question next, say 'a

grave-maker: 'the houses that he makes last till

doomsday. Go, get thee to Yaughan: fetch me a

stoup of liquor.

Exit Second Clown
He digs and sings

In youth, when I did love, did love,

Methought it was very sweet,

To contract, O, the time, for, ah, my behove,

O, methought, there was nothing meet.

HAMLET
Has this fellow no feeling of his business, that he

sings at grave-making?

HORATIO
Custom hath made it in him a property of easiness.

HAMLET
'Tis e'en so: the hand of little employment hath

the daintier sense.

First Clown
[Sings]

But age, with his stealing steps,

Hath claw'd me in his clutch,

And hath shipped me intil the land,

As if I had never been such.

Throws up a skull

HAMLET
That skull had a tongue in it, and could sing once:

how the knave jowls it to the ground, as if it were

Cain's jaw-bone, that did the first murder! It

might be the pate of a politician, which this ass

now o'er-reaches; one that would circumvent God,

might it not?

HORATIO
It might, my lord.

HAMLET
Or of a courtier; which could say 'Good morrow,

sweet lord! How dost thou, good lord?' This might

be my lord such-a-one, that praised my lord

such-a-one's horse, when he meant to beg it; might it not?

HORATIO
Ay, my lord.

HAMLET
Why, e'en so: and now my Lady Worm's; chapless, and

knocked about the mazzard with a sexton's spade:

here's fine revolution, an we had the trick to

see't. Did these bones cost no more the breeding,

but to play at loggats with 'em? mine ache to think on't.

First Clown
[Sings]

A pick-axe, and a spade, a spade,

For and a shrouding sheet:

O, a pit of clay for to be made

For such a guest is meet.

Throws up another skull

HAMLET
There's another: why may not that be the skull of a

lawyer? Where be his quiddities now, his quillets,

his cases, his tenures, and his tricks? why does he

suffer this rude knave now to knock him about the

sconce with a dirty shovel, and will not tell him of

his action of battery? Hum! This fellow might be

in's time a great buyer of land, with his statutes,

his recognizances, his fines, his double vouchers,

his recoveries: is this the fine of his fines, and

the recovery of his recoveries, to have his fine

pate full of fine dirt? will his vouchers vouch him

no more of his purchases, and double ones too, than

the length and breadth of a pair of indentures? The

very conveyances of his lands will hardly lie in

this box; and must the inheritor himself have no more, ha?

HORATIO
Not a jot more, my lord.

HAMLET
Is not parchment made of sheepskins?

HORATIO
Ay, my lord, and of calf-skins too.

HAMLET
They are sheep and calves which seek out assurance

in that. I will speak to this fellow. Whose

grave's this, sirrah?

First Clown
Mine, sir.

Sings
O, a pit of clay for to be made

For such a guest is meet.

HAMLET
I think it be thine, indeed; for thou liest in't.

First Clown
You lie out on't, sir, and therefore it is not

yours: for my part, I do not lie in't, and yet it is mine.

HAMLET
'Thou dost lie in't, to be in't and say it is thine:

'tis for the dead, not for the quick; therefore thou liest.

First Clown
'Tis a quick lie, sir; 'twill away gain, from me to

you.

HAMLET
What man dost thou dig it for?

First Clown
For no man, sir.

HAMLET
What woman, then?

First Clown
For none, neither.

HAMLET
Who is to be buried in't?

First Clown
One that was a woman, sir; but, rest her soul, she's dead.

HAMLET
How absolute the knave is! we must speak by the

card, or equivocation will undo us. By the Lord,

Horatio, these three years I have taken a note of

it; the age is grown so picked that the toe of the

peasant comes so near the heel of the courtier, he

gaffs his kibe. How long hast thou been a

grave-maker?

First Clown
Of all the days i' the year, I came to't that day

that our last king Hamlet overcame Fortinbras.

HAMLET
How long is that since?

First Clown
Cannot you tell that? every fool can tell that: it

was the very day that young Hamlet was born; he that

is mad, and sent into England.

HAMLET
Ay, marry, why was he sent into England?

First Clown
Why, because he was mad: he shall recover his wits

there; or, if he do not, it's no great matter there.

HAMLET
Why?

First Clown
'Twill, a not be seen in him there; there the men

are as mad as he.

HAMLET
How came he mad?

First Clown
Very strangely, they say.

HAMLET
How strangely?

First Clown
Faith, e'en with losing his wits.

HAMLET
Upon what ground?

First Clown
Why, here in Denmark: I have been sexton here, man

and boy, thirty years.

HAMLET
How long will a man lie i' the earth ere he rot?

First Clown
I' faith, if he be not rotten before he die--as we

have many pocky corses now-a-days, that will scarce

hold the laying in--he will last you some eight year

or nine year: a tanner will last you nine year.

HAMLET
Why he more than another?

First Clown
Why, sir, his hide is so tanned with his trade, that

he will keep out water a great while; and your water

is a sore decayer of your whoreson dead body.

Here's a skull now; this skull has lain in the earth

three and twenty years.

HAMLET
Whose was it?

First Clown
A whoreson mad fellow's it was: whose do you think it was?

HAMLET
Nay, I know not.

First Clown

A pestilence on him for a mad rogue! a' poured a

flagon of Rhenish on my head once. This same skull,

sir, was Yorick's skull, the king's jester.

HAMLET

This?

First Clown

E'en that.

HAMLET

Let me see.

Takes the skull

Alas, poor Yorick! I knew him, Horatio: a fellow

of infinite jest, of most excellent fancy: he hath

borne me on his back a thousand times; and now, how

abhorred in my imagination it is! my gorge rims at

it. Here hung those lips that I have kissed I know

not how oft. Where be your gibes now? your

gambols? your songs? your flashes of merriment,

that were wont to set the table on a roar? Not one

now, to mock your own grinning? quite chap-fallen?

Now get you to my lady's chamber, and tell her, let

her paint an inch thick, to this favour she must

come; make her laugh at that. Prithee, Horatio, tell

me one thing.

HORATIO

What's that, my lord?

HAMLET

Dost thou think Alexander looked o' this fashion i'

the earth?

HORATIO

E'en so.

HAMLET

And smelt so? pah!

Puts down the skull

HORATIO

E'en so, my lord.

HAMLET

To what base uses we may return, Horatio! Why may

not imagination trace the noble dust of Alexander,

till he find it stopping a bung-hole?

HORATIO

'Twere to consider too curiously, to consider so.

HAMLET

No, faith, not a jot; but to follow him thither with

modesty enough, and likelihood to lead it: as

thus: Alexander died, Alexander was buried,

Alexander returneth into dust; the dust is earth; of

earth we make loam; and why of that loam, whereto he

was converted, might they not stop a beer-barrel?

Imperious Caesar, dead and turn'd to clay,

Might stop a hole to keep the wind away:

O, that that earth, which kept the world in awe,

Should patch a wall to expel the winter flaw!

But soft! but soft! aside: here comes the king.

Enter Priest, & c. in procession; the Corpse of OPHELIA, LAERTES

and Mourners following; KING CLAUDIUS, QUEEN GERTRUDE,

their trains, & c

The queen, the courtiers: who is this they follow?

And with such maimed rites? This doth betoken

The corse they follow did with desperate hand

Fordo its own life: 'twas of some estate.

Couch we awhile, and mark.

Retiring with HORATIO

LAERTES
What ceremony else?

HAMLET
That is Laertes,

A very noble youth: mark.

LAERTES
What ceremony else?

First Priest
Her obsequies have been as far enlarged

As we have warrantise: her death was doubtful;

And, but that great command o'ersways the order,

She should in ground unsanctified have lodged

Till the last trumpet: for charitable prayers,

Shards, flints and pebbles should be thrown on her;

Yet here she is allow'd her virgin crants,

Her maiden strewments and the bringing home

Of bell and burial.

LAERTES
Must there no more be done?

First Priest
No more be done:

We should profane the service of the dead

To sing a requiem and such rest to her

As to peace-parted souls.

LAERTES
Lay her i' the earth:

And from her fair and unpolluted flesh

May violets spring! I tell thee, churlish priest,

A ministering angel shall my sister be,

When thou liest howling.

HAMLET
What, the fair Ophelia!

QUEEN GERTRUDE
Sweets to the sweet: farewell!

Scattering flowers

I hoped thou shouldst have been my Hamlet's wife;

I thought thy bride-bed to have deck'd, sweet maid,

And not have strew'd thy grave.

LAERTES
O, treble woe

Fall ten times treble on that cursed head,

Whose wicked deed thy most ingenious sense

Deprived thee of! Hold off the earth awhile,

Till I have caught her once more in mine arms:

Leaps into the grave

Now pile your dust upon the quick and dead,

Till of this flat a mountain you have made,

To o'ertop old Pelion, or the skyish head

Of blue Olympus.

HAMLET
[Advancing] What is he whose grief

Bears such an emphasis? whose phrase of sorrow

Conjures the wandering stars, and makes them stand

Like wonder-wounded hearers? This is I,

Hamlet the Dane.

Leaps into the grave

LAERTES
The devil take thy soul!

Grappling with him

HAMLET
Thou pray'st not well.

I prithee, take thy fingers from my throat;

For, though I am not splenitive and rash,

Yet have I something in me dangerous,

Which let thy wiseness fear: hold off thy hand.

KING CLAUDIUS
Pluck them asunder.

QUEEN GERTRUDE
Hamlet, Hamlet!

All
Gentlemen,--

HORATIO
Good my lord, be quiet.

The Attendants part them, and they come out of the grave

HAMLET
Why I will fight with him upon this theme

Until my eyelids will no longer wag.

QUEEN GERTRUDE
O my son, what theme?

HAMLET
I loved Ophelia: forty thousand brothers

Could not, with all their quantity of love,

Make up my sum. What wilt thou do for her?

KING CLAUDIUS
O, he is mad, Laertes.

QUEEN GERTRUDE
For love of God, forbear him.

HAMLET
'Swounds, show me what thou'lt do:

Woo't weep? woo't fight? woo't fast? woo't tear thyself?

Woo't drink up eisel? eat a crocodile?

I'll do't. Dost thou come here to whine?

To outface me with leaping in her grave?

Be buried quick with her, and so will I:

And, if thou prate of mountains, let them throw

Millions of acres on us, till our ground,

Singeing his pate against the burning zone,

Make Ossa like a wart! Nay, an thou'lt mouth,

I'll rant as well as thou.

QUEEN GERTRUDE
This is mere madness:

And thus awhile the fit will work on him;

Anon, as patient as the female dove,

When that her golden couplets are disclosed,

His silence will sit drooping.

HAMLET
Hear you, sir;

What is the reason that you use me thus?

I loved you ever: but it is no matter;

Let Hercules himself do what he may,

The cat will mew and dog will have his day.

Exit

KING CLAUDIUS
I pray you, good Horatio, wait upon him.

Exit HORATIO

To LAERTES

Strengthen your patience in our last night's speech;

We'll put the matter to the present push.

Good Gertrude, set some watch over your son.

This grave shall have a living monument:

An hour of quiet shortly shall we see;

Till then, in patience our proceeding be.

Exeunt

<u>*NOTES*</u>

SCENE II. A hall in the castle.

Enter HAMLET and HORATIO

HAMLET
So much for this, sir: now shall you see the other;

You do remember all the circumstance?

HORATIO
Remember it, my lord?

HAMLET
Sir, in my heart there was a kind of fighting,

That would not let me sleep: methought I lay

Worse than the mutines in the bilboes. Rashly,

And praised be rashness for it, let us know,

Our indiscretion sometimes serves us well,

When our deep plots do pall: and that should teach us

There's a divinity that shapes our ends,

Rough-hew them how we will,--

HORATIO
That is most certain.

HAMLET
Up from my cabin,

My sea-gown scarf'd about me, in the dark

Groped I to find out them; had my desire.

Finger'd their packet, and in fine withdrew

To mine own room again; making so bold,

My fears forgetting manners, to unseal

Their grand commission; where I found, Horatio,--

O royal knavery!--an exact command,

Larded with many several sorts of reasons

Importing Denmark's health and England's too,

With, ho! such bugs and goblins in my life,

That, on the supervise, no leisure bated,

No, not to stay the grinding of the axe,

My head should be struck off.

HORATIO
Is't possible?

HAMLET
Here's the commission: read it at more leisure.

But wilt thou hear me how I did proceed?

HORATIO
I beseech you.

HAMLET
Being thus be-netted round with villanies,--

Ere I could make a prologue to my brains,

They had begun the play--I sat me down,

Devised a new commission, wrote it fair:

I once did hold it, as our statists do,

A baseness to write fair and labour'd much

How to forget that learning, but, sir, now

It did me yeoman's service: wilt thou know

The effect of what I wrote?

HORATIO
Ay, good my lord.

HAMLET
An earnest conjuration from the king,

As England was his faithful tributary,

As love between them like the palm might flourish,

As peace should stiff her wheaten garland wear

And stand a comma 'tween their amities,

And many such-like 'As'es of great charge,

That, on the view and knowing of these contents,

Without debatement further, more or less,

He should the bearers put to sudden death,

Not shriving-time allow'd.

HORATIO
How was this seal'd?

HAMLET
Why, even in that was heaven ordinant.

I had my father's signet in my purse,

Which was the model of that Danish seal;

Folded the writ up in form of the other,

Subscribed it, gave't the impression, placed it safely,

The changeling never known. Now, the next day

Was our sea-fight; and what to this was sequent

Thou know'st already.

HORATIO
So Guildenstern and Rosencrantz go to't.

HAMLET
Why, man, they did make love to this employment;

They are not near my conscience; their defeat

Does by their own insinuation grow:

'Tis dangerous when the baser nature comes

Between the pass and fell incensed points

Of mighty opposites.

HORATIO
Why, what a king is this!

HAMLET
Does it not, think'st thee, stand me now upon--

He that hath kill'd my king and whored my mother,

Popp'd in between the election and my hopes,

Thrown out his angle for my proper life,

And with such cozenage--is't not perfect conscience,

To quit him with this arm? and is't not to be damn'd,

To let this canker of our nature come

In further evil?

HORATIO
It must be shortly known to him from England

What is the issue of the business there.

HAMLET

It will be short: the interim is mine;

And a man's life's no more than to say 'One.'

But I am very sorry, good Horatio,

That to Laertes I forgot myself;

For, by the image of my cause, I see

The portraiture of his: I'll court his favours.

But, sure, the bravery of his grief did put me

Into a towering passion.

HORATIO

Peace! who comes here?

Enter OSRIC

OSRIC

Your lordship is right welcome back to Denmark.

HAMLET

I humbly thank you, sir. Dost know this water-fly?

HORATIO

No, my good lord.

HAMLET

Thy state is the more gracious; for 'tis a vice to

know him. He hath much land, and fertile: let a

beast be lord of beasts, and his crib shall stand at

the king's mess: 'tis a chough; but, as I say,

spacious in the possession of dirt.

OSRIC

Sweet lord, if your lordship were at leisure, I

should impart a thing to you from his majesty.

HAMLET
I will receive it, sir, with all diligence of

spirit. Put your bonnet to his right use; 'tis for the head.

OSRIC
I thank your lordship, it is very hot.

HAMLET
No, believe me, 'tis very cold; the wind is

northerly.

OSRIC
It is indifferent cold, my lord, indeed.

HAMLET
But yet methinks it is very sultry and hot for my

complexion.

OSRIC
Exceedingly, my lord; it is very sultry,--as

'twere,--I cannot tell how. But, my lord, his

majesty bade me signify to you that he has laid a

great wager on your head: sir, this is the matter,--

HAMLET
I beseech you, remember--

HAMLET moves him to put on his hat

OSRIC
Nay, good my lord; for mine ease, in good faith.

Sir, here is newly come to court Laertes; believe

me, an absolute gentleman, full of most excellent

differences, of very soft society and great showing:

indeed, to speak feelingly of him, he is the card or

calendar of gentry, for you shall find in him the

continent of what part a gentleman would see.

HAMLET
Sir, his definement suffers no perdition in you;

though, I know, to divide him inventorially would

dizzy the arithmetic of memory, and yet but yaw

neither, in respect of his quick sail. But, in the

verity of extolment, I take him to be a soul of

great article; and his infusion of such dearth and

rareness, as, to make true diction of him, his

semblable is his mirror; and who else would trace

him, his umbrage, nothing more.

OSRIC
Your lordship speaks most infallibly of him.

HAMLET
The concernancy, sir? why do we wrap the gentleman

in our more rawer breath?

OSRIC
Sir?

HORATIO
Is't not possible to understand in another tongue?

You will do't, sir, really.

HAMLET
What imports the nomination of this gentleman?

OSRIC
Of Laertes?

HORATIO
His purse is empty already; all's golden words are spent.

HAMLET
Of him, sir.

OSRIC
I know you are not ignorant--

HAMLET
I would you did, sir; yet, in faith, if you did,

it would not much approve me. Well, sir?

OSRIC
You are not ignorant of what excellence Laertes is--

HAMLET
I dare not confess that, lest I should compare with

him in excellence; but, to know a man well, were to

know himself.

OSRIC
I mean, sir, for his weapon; but in the imputation

laid on him by them, in his meed he's unfellowed.

HAMLET
What's his weapon?

OSRIC
Rapier and dagger.

HAMLET
That's two of his weapons: but, well.

OSRIC

The king, sir, hath wagered with him six Barbary

horses: against the which he has imponed, as I take

it, six French rapiers and poniards, with their

assigns, as girdle, hangers, and so: three of the

carriages, in faith, are very dear to fancy, very

responsive to the hilts, most delicate carriages,

and of very liberal conceit.

HAMLET

What call you the carriages?

HORATIO

I knew you must be edified by the margent ere you had done.

OSRIC

The carriages, sir, are the hangers.

HAMLET

The phrase would be more german to the matter, if we

could carry cannon by our sides: I would it might

be hangers till then. But, on: six Barbary horses

against six French swords, their assigns, and three

liberal-conceited carriages; that's the French bet

against the Danish. Why is this 'imponed,' as you call it?

OSRIC

The king, sir, hath laid, that in a dozen passes

between yourself and him, he shall not exceed you

three hits: he hath laid on twelve for nine; and it

would come to immediate trial, if your lordship

would vouchsafe the answer.

HAMLET
How if I answer 'no'?

OSRIC
I mean, my lord, the opposition of your person in trial.

HAMLET
Sir, I will walk here in the hall: if it please his

majesty, 'tis the breathing time of day with me; let

the foils be brought, the gentleman willing, and the

king hold his purpose, I will win for him an I can;

if not, I will gain nothing but my shame and the odd hits.

OSRIC
Shall I re-deliver you e'en so?

HAMLET
To this effect, sir; after what flourish your nature will.

OSRIC
I commend my duty to your lordship.

HAMLET
Yours, yours.

Exit OSRIC
He does well to commend it himself; there are no

tongues else for's turn.

HORATIO
This lapwing runs away with the shell on his head.

HAMLET
He did comply with his dug, before he sucked it.

Thus has he--and many more of the same bevy that I

know the dressy age dotes on--only got the tune of

the time and outward habit of encounter; a kind of

yesty collection, which carries them through and

through the most fond and winnowed opinions; and do

but blow them to their trial, the bubbles are out.

Enter a Lord

Lord
My lord, his majesty commended him to you by young

Osric, who brings back to him that you attend him in

the hall: he sends to know if your pleasure hold to

play with Laertes, or that you will take longer time.

HAMLET
I am constant to my purpose; they follow the king's

pleasure: if his fitness speaks, mine is ready; now

or whensoever, provided I be so able as now.

Lord
The king and queen and all are coming down.

HAMLET
In happy time.

Lord
The queen desires you to use some gentle

entertainment to Laertes before you fall to play.

HAMLET
She well instructs me.

Exit Lord

HORATIO
You will lose this wager, my lord.

HAMLET
I do not think so: since he went into France, I

have been in continual practise: I shall win at the

odds. But thou wouldst not think how ill all's here

about my heart: but it is no matter.

HORATIO
Nay, good my lord,--

HAMLET
It is but foolery; but it is such a kind of

gain-giving, as would perhaps trouble a woman.

HORATIO
If your mind dislike any thing, obey it: I will

forestall their repair hither, and say you are not

fit.

HAMLET
Not a whit, we defy augury: there's a special

providence in the fall of a sparrow. If it be now,

'tis not to come; if it be not to come, it will be

now; if it be not now, yet it will come: the

readiness is all: since no man has aught of what he

leaves, what is't to leave betimes?

*Enter KING CLAUDIUS, QUEEN GERTRUDE, LAERTES, Lords,
OSRIC, and Attendants with foils, & c*

KING CLAUDIUS
Come, Hamlet, come, and take this hand from me.

KING CLAUDIUS puts LAERTES' hand into HAMLET's

HAMLET
Give me your pardon, sir: I've done you wrong;

But pardon't, as you are a gentleman.

This presence knows,

And you must needs have heard, how I am punish'd

With sore distraction. What I have done,

That might your nature, honour and exception

Roughly awake, I here proclaim was madness.

Was't Hamlet wrong'd Laertes? Never Hamlet:

If Hamlet from himself be ta'en away,

And when he's not himself does wrong Laertes,

Then Hamlet does it not, Hamlet denies it.

Who does it, then? His madness: if't be so,

Hamlet is of the faction that is wrong'd;

His madness is poor Hamlet's enemy.

Sir, in this audience,

Let my disclaiming from a purposed evil

Free me so far in your most generous thoughts,

That I have shot mine arrow o'er the house,

And hurt my brother.

LAERTES

I am satisfied in nature,

Whose motive, in this case, should stir me most

To my revenge: but in my terms of honour

I stand aloof; and will no reconcilement,

Till by some elder masters, of known honour,

I have a voice and precedent of peace,

To keep my name ungored. But till that time,

I do receive your offer'd love like love,

And will not wrong it.

HAMLET

I embrace it freely;

And will this brother's wager frankly play.

Give us the foils. Come on.

LAERTES

Come, one for me.

HAMLET

I'll be your foil, Laertes: in mine ignorance

Your skill shall, like a star i' the darkest night,

Stick fiery off indeed.

LAERTES

You mock me, sir.

HAMLET

No, by this hand.

KING CLAUDIUS
Give them the foils, young Osric. Cousin Hamlet,

You know the wager?

HAMLET
Very well, my lord

Your grace hath laid the odds o' the weaker side.

KING CLAUDIUS
I do not fear it; I have seen you both:

But since he is better'd, we have therefore odds.

LAERTES
This is too heavy, let me see another.

HAMLET
This likes me well. These foils have all a length?

They prepare to play

OSRIC
Ay, my good lord.

KING CLAUDIUS
Set me the stoops of wine upon that table.

If Hamlet give the first or second hit,

Or quit in answer of the third exchange,

Let all the battlements their ordnance fire:

The king shall drink to Hamlet's better breath;

And in the cup an union shall he throw,

Richer than that which four successive kings

In Denmark's crown have worn. Give me the cups;

And let the kettle to the trumpet speak,

The trumpet to the cannoneer without,

The cannons to the heavens, the heavens to earth,

'Now the king dunks to Hamlet.' Come, begin:

And you, the judges, bear a wary eye.

HAMLET
Come on, sir.

LAERTES
Come, my lord.

They play
HAMLET
One.

LAERTES
No.

HAMLET
Judgment.

OSRIC
A hit, a very palpable hit.

LAERTES
Well; again.

KING CLAUDIUS
Stay; give me drink. Hamlet, this pearl is thine;

Here's to thy health.

Trumpets sound, and cannon shot off within

Give him the cup.

HAMLET
I'll play this bout first; set it by awhile. Come.

They play

Another hit; what say you?

LAERTES
A touch, a touch, I do confess.

KING CLAUDIUS
Our son shall win.

QUEEN GERTRUDE
He's fat, and scant of breath.

Here, Hamlet, take my napkin, rub thy brows;

The queen carouses to thy fortune, Hamlet.

HAMLET
Good madam!

KING CLAUDIUS
Gertrude, do not drink.

QUEEN GERTRUDE
I will, my lord; I pray you, pardon me.

KING CLAUDIUS
[Aside] It is the poison'd cup: it is too late.

HAMLET
I dare not drink yet, madam; by and by.

QUEEN GERTRUDE
Come, let me wipe thy face.

LAERTES
My lord, I'll hit him now.

KING CLAUDIUS
I do not think't.

LAERTES
[Aside] And yet 'tis almost 'gainst my conscience.

HAMLET
Come, for the third, Laertes: you but dally;

I pray you, pass with your best violence;

I am afeard you make a wanton of me.

LAERTES
Say you so? come on.

They play

OSRIC
Nothing, neither way.

LAERTES
Have at you now!

LAERTES wounds HAMLET; then in scuffling, they change rapiers, and HAMLET wounds LAERTES

KING CLAUDIUS
Part them; they are incensed.

HAMLET
Nay, come, again.

QUEEN GERTRUDE falls

OSRIC
Look to the queen there, ho!

HORATIO
They bleed on both sides. How is it, my lord?

OSRIC
How is't, Laertes?

LAERTES
Why, as a woodcock to mine own springe, Osric;

I am justly kill'd with mine own treachery.

HAMLET
How does the queen?

KING CLAUDIUS
She swounds to see them bleed.

QUEEN GERTRUDE
No, no, the drink, the drink,--O my dear Hamlet,--

The drink, the drink! I am poison'd.

Dies

HAMLET
O villany! Ho! let the door be lock'd:

Treachery! Seek it out.

LAERTES
It is here, Hamlet: Hamlet, thou art slain;

No medicine in the world can do thee good;

In thee there is not half an hour of life;

The treacherous instrument is in thy hand,

Unbated and envenom'd: the foul practise

Hath turn'd itself on me lo, here I lie,

Never to rise again: thy mother's poison'd:

I can no more: the king, the king's to blame.

HAMLET
The point!--envenom'd too!

Then, venom, to thy work.

Stabs KING CLAUDIUS

All
Treason! treason!

KING CLAUDIUS
O, yet defend me, friends; I am but hurt.

HAMLET
Here, thou incestuous, murderous, damned Dane,

Drink off this potion. Is thy union here?

Follow my mother.

KING CLAUDIUS dies

LAERTES
He is justly served;

It is a poison temper'd by himself.

Exchange forgiveness with me, noble Hamlet:

Mine and my father's death come not upon thee,

Nor thine on me.

Dies

HAMLET
Heaven make thee free of it! I follow thee.

I am dead, Horatio. Wretched queen, adieu!

You that look pale and tremble at this chance,

That are but mutes or audience to this act,

Had I but time--as this fell sergeant, death,

Is strict in his arrest--O, I could tell you--

But let it be. Horatio, I am dead;

Thou livest; report me and my cause aright

To the unsatisfied.

HORATIO
Never believe it:

I am more an antique Roman than a Dane:

Here's yet some liquor left.

HAMLET
As thou'rt a man,

Give me the cup: let go; by heaven, I'll have't.

O good Horatio, what a wounded name,

Things standing thus unknown, shall live behind me!

If thou didst ever hold me in thy heart

Absent thee from felicity awhile,

And in this harsh world draw thy breath in pain,

To tell my story.

March afar off, and shot within

What warlike noise is this?

OSRIC
Young Fortinbras, with conquest come from Poland,

To the ambassadors of England gives

This warlike volley.

HAMLET
O, I die, Horatio;

The potent poison quite o'er-crows my spirit:

I cannot live to hear the news from England;

But I do prophesy the election lights

On Fortinbras: he has my dying voice;

So tell him, with the occurrents, more and less,

Which have solicited. The rest is silence.

Dies

HORATIO
Now cracks a noble heart. Good night sweet prince:

And flights of angels sing thee to thy rest!

Why does the drum come hither?

March within

Enter FORTINBRAS, the English Ambassadors, and others

PRINCE FORTINBRAS
Where is this sight?

HORATIO
What is it ye would see?

If aught of woe or wonder, cease your search.

PRINCE FORTINBRAS
This quarry cries on havoc. O proud death,

What feast is toward in thine eternal cell,

That thou so many princes at a shot

So bloodily hast struck?

First Ambassador
The sight is dismal;

And our affairs from England come too late:

The ears are senseless that should give us hearing,

To tell him his commandment is fulfill'd,

That Rosencrantz and Guildenstern are dead:

Where should we have our thanks?

HORATIO
Not from his mouth,

Had it the ability of life to thank you:

He never gave commandment for their death.

But since, so jump upon this bloody question,

You from the Polack wars, and you from England,

Are here arrived give order that these bodies

High on a stage be placed to the view;

And let me speak to the yet unknowing world

How these things came about: so shall you hear

Of carnal, bloody, and unnatural acts,

Of accidental judgments, casual slaughters,

Of deaths put on by cunning and forced cause,

And, in this upshot, purposes mistook

Fall'n on the inventors' reads: all this can I

Truly deliver.

PRINCE FORTINBRAS
Let us haste to hear it,

And call the noblest to the audience.

For me, with sorrow I embrace my fortune:

I have some rights of memory in this kingdom,

Which now to claim my vantage doth invite me.

HORATIO
Of that I shall have also cause to speak,

And from his mouth whose voice will draw on more;

But let this same be presently perform'd,

Even while men's minds are wild; lest more mischance

On plots and errors, happen.

PRINCE FORTINBRAS
Let four captains

Bear Hamlet, like a soldier, to the stage;

For he was likely, had he been put on,

To have proved most royally: and, for his passage,

The soldiers' music and the rites of war

Speak loudly for him.

Take up the bodies: such a sight as this

Becomes the field, but here shows much amiss.

Go, bid the soldiers shoot.

A dead march. Exeunt, bearing off the dead bodies; after which a peal of ordnance is shot off

<u>*NOTES*</u>

NOTES

NOTES

Made in the USA
Columbia, SC
07 January 2023

75766026R00135